Indigenous Schooling in the Modern World

Education, Culture, and Society

Founding Editor

Bernardo Gallegos†

Editorial Board

Ming Fang He (*Georgia Southern University, USA*)
Paula Groves-Price (*Washington State University, USA*)
Isabel Nuñez (*Indiana University/Purdue University, Fort Wayne, USA*)
Rodolfo Palma-Rojo (*Universidad Nacional Autónoma de Mexico, Mexico*)
William Schubert (*Emeritus, University of Illinois at Chicago, USA*)
Mette Marie Wacher Rodarte (*Instituto Nacional de Antropología e Historia, Mexico*)

VOLUME 3

The titles published in this series are listed at *brill.com/ecas*

Indigenous Schooling in the Modern World

Education, Knowledge and Liberation for All Citizens

By

Neil Hooley, Oksana Razoumova and Lois Peeler

BRILL

LEIDEN | BOSTON

Cover illustration: River landscape with wattle, photograph by David Callow

All chapters in this book have undergone peer review.

The Library of Congress Cataloging-in-Publication Data is available online at http://catalog.loc.gov

Typeface for the Latin, Greek, and Cyrillic scripts: "Brill". See and download: brill.com/brill-typeface.

ISSN 2590-0005
ISBN 978-90-04-50540-7 (paperback)
ISBN 978-90-04-50541-4 (hardback)
ISBN 978-90-04-50542-1 (e-book)

Copyright 2021 by Koninklijke Brill NV, Leiden, The Netherlands.
Koninklijke Brill NV incorporates the imprints Brill, Brill Nijhoff, Brill Hotei, Brill Schöningh, Brill Fink, Brill mentis, Vandenhoeck & Ruprecht, Böhlau Verlag and V&R Unipress.
All rights reserved. No part of this publication may be reproduced, translated, stored in a retrieval system, or transmitted in any form or by any means, electronic, mechanical, photocopying, recording or otherwise, without prior written permission from the publisher. Requests for re-use and/or translations must be addressed to Koninklijke Brill NV via brill.com or copyright.com.

This book is printed on acid-free paper and produced in a sustainable manner.

The nexus between cultural ways of knowing, scientific discoveries, economic impulses and imperial power enabled the West to make ideological claims to having a superior civilisation. The 'idea' of the West became a reality when it was re-presented back to Indigenous nations through colonisation. By the Nineteenth Century, colonisation not only meant the imposition of Western authority over Indigenous lands, Indigenous modes of production and Indigenous law and government, but the imposition of Western authority over all aspects of Indigenous knowledges, languages and cultures.

LINDA TUHIWAI SMITH (1999, p. 64)

Contents

Preface IX
Acknowledgements XIII
List of Figures and Tables XIV
About the Authors XV
Terminology XVII

1 **Global Trends and the Struggle for Indigeneity** 1
   1   What It Means to Be Indigenous 1
   2   Decolonising Education and Knowledge 4
   3   Identity within Neoliberalism 5
   4   Living between Worlds 8
   5   Sovereignty and Self-Determination 10
   6   Prospects for Indigenisation 11
   7   Diversity and Harmony in Our Time 14
   8   Uluru Statement from the Heart 17
   9   Excursus 1: Sand and Sky 18

2 **Case Study: Worawa Aboriginal College** 19
   1   Living and Learning Together 19
   2   Commitment to Education, Culture, Language and Wellbeing 21
   3   Community-Based Expansion of Student Leadership Development Opportunities 22
   4   Culture Curriculum, Contemporary and Traditional 23
   5   Curriculum, a Holistic Experience 28
   6   Bringing Peoples and Ideas Together 31
   7   Indigenous Knowledge as Cultural Practice 32
   8   Knowledge Exemplars – Two-way Inquiry Learning 34
   9   Excursus 2: Indigenous Science, or Not 37

3 **Experience through the Arts** 39
   1   Picasso and Namatjira 40
   2   School Education and the Arts 42
   3   Praxis Philosophy of Arts 46
   4   Excursus 3: Tower Hill 48

4 **Redefining School Mathematics as Philosophy of Practice** 49
   1   Indigenous Approaches to School Mathematics 50

	2	Ethnomathematics, a Cultural View of Mathematics 54
	3	Wittgenstein and the Foundations of Mathematics 57
	4	Excursus 4: Rock Pools 60
5	**Language Connections with the World** 62	
	1	Formations of Society, Language, Thought 62
	2	Perspective of Indigenous Language 66
	3	Language of Visual Thought and Expression 70
	4	Reflective Interlude 72
	5	Excursus 5: A Process of Eyes Opened Wide 73
6	**Education as Philosophy of Pragmatism and Practice** 75	
	1	Coming to Practice 75
	2	Background to Pragmatism and Pragmatists 80
	3	Practice, Praxis and Signature Pedagogies 83
	4	Discursive Curriculum 86
	5	Excursus 6: Meaning in Engines 89
7	**Citizen Education** 91	
	1	Education as Philosophy of Practice 91
	2	Assessment, the 'Hard Question' of Education 94
	3	Citizen Knowledge, Truth and Freedom 99
	4	Excursus 7: International Friendship 103
8	**The Invincible Spirit, Defining the Future** 105	

References 113
Index 120

Preface

Indigenous education constitutes one of the great unresolved struggles for the advancement of moral life around the world. It does not exist in grand isolation, but is immersed in the major political, economic and cultural trends of the era, national and international. Indigenous peoples live in different countries where such trends are applied differently, where various forms of colonialism and racism still exist and where they may be a smaller or larger proportion of the population. In each case, a range of strategies need to be formulated to enable participation in the dominant society and economy and which contribute to social justice and peace. For those societies that espouse democratic intent, education is a key strategic component of providing information and knowledge for all participants regardless of socio-cultural background and of encouraging discussion and critique of social processes that form the basis of daily existence. Accordingly, Dewey's elaboration provides guidance for the nature of equitable and inclusive education, when he states that 'A democracy is more than a form of government, it is primarily a mode of associated living, of conjoint communicated experience' (Dewey, 1916, p. 87). More than this, each generation must discover and experience democracy for itself. Within this philosophical framework, primary schooling can be conceived as providing broad experience for language and learning development and emphasises the care and safety of young children. Secondary schooling becomes more specific in arranging contact with different forms of knowledge and requires more abstract thought in senior years. Under these conditions, all Indigenous children should be able to be included in systems of education that are developed with philosophical integrity and respect. Unfortunately, most countries of the world have found this very difficult to achieve.

This book has been written to support the formal education of all Indigenous children who live in different circumstances. It takes Indigenous philosophy, learning and knowledge as its starting point, while recognising that in many colonial and post-colonial circumstances, Indigenous history, culture and language may not be valued. For this reason, Indigenous and non-Indigenous theorists and authors are included to demonstrate the recognised links between Indigenous and non-Indigenous understandings and practices of culture, knowledge and learning and therefore common approaches to formal education. Chapters are arranged in an integrated fashion to discuss issues regarding global political and economic influences and the notion of what it means to participate fully in society. Following Chapter 1 that outlines some global and contextual issues regarding Indigeneity, sovereignty and self-determination and the dominance of neoliberalism, Chapter 2 discusses Indigenous education in detail with a case study of Worawa Aboriginal College, Australia. Features of the educational program at Worawa are described including principles of teaching and learning that can be adopted by Indigenous and non-Indigenous schools alike. Chapters 3, 4 and 5 discuss curriculum issues of arts, mathematics and language identifying various forms of activity and practice considered from a pragmatist perspective. Human language is a common thread that runs throughout this discussion, enabling ideas and understandings to be constructed, expressed and reformulated as encounters with the social and physical worlds accumulate. Chapter 6 draws key ideas from previous chapters together and introduces discussion of pragmatist philosophy that is seen as an appropriate means of reconciling Indigenous and non-Indigenous knowledges for application by schools. Principles of learning that include storey telling, learning by doing, emphasising language experience and respecting community culture fit nicely within a pragmatist frame. Chapter 7 summarises and proposes a draft curriculum design that can realistically be considered by schools around the world for culturally-inclusive practices and where community and personal knowledges form the basis of new learning. We conclude the book with Chapter 8, the transcript of a speech by Aunty Lois Peeler, who raises philosophical, cultural and educational issues regarding her personal experiences and those of establishing an Indigenous college in Australia. Through her warm expression, Aunty Lois demonstrates life-long and heart-felt commitment towards 'walking together' with all peoples for peace and justice. *Indigenous Schooling in the Modern World* is a book for practitioners where practice and the theorising of practice occurs as one, simultaneously. Figure 1 shows this relationship.

There is a distinction to be made between education in the general sense for humans and formal schooling, understood as procedures to impart specified information, facts and ideas for children. Taking the famous statement by Dewey (1897) as a guide, that education, 'is a process of living and not a

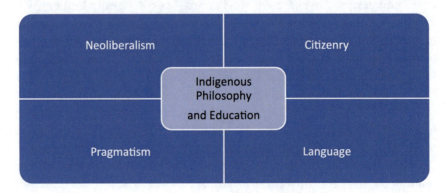

FIGURE 1   Organisational outline of chapters and main themes

preparation for future living,' means that education is a process whereby all humans interact with their environments, resolve issues that arise and decide what should be done next. Education therefore is a natural process for the human species, they learn to be human. On the other hand, institutionalised schooling in most cases is an unnatural set of procedures for children to accept what is provided as being important and accurate. For all families and children and in particular Indigenous children, this notion of formal schooling can therefore establish serious and difficult contradictions between school, home and community. There is a world view of Indigenous knowledge and learning, where Indigenous education needs to be seen as referring to the ways in which cultures educate or shape perspective and influence action of cultural participants, where learning is holistic and an active child and community process. Bringing Indigenous understandings of knowledge and learning into a respectful relationship with formal education/schooling systems of the dominant society, will benefit Indigenous and non-Indigenous children alike. Ultimately, Indigenous inequality in the dominant society can be combatted by education/schooling in this way. That is, by assisting students to be both culturally confident and experienced and to be successful in the regular school curriculum, so that the difficulties and challenges of social life can be traversed. Inequality is a political and economic matter, but strengthening education/schooling participation for Indigenous peoples as discussed above, provides a personal and community framework to combat its pernicious character.

Policy documents regarding Indigenous education can usually be found at the international and national levels. For example, the Declaration on the Rights of Indigenous Peoples (UN, 2019b) contains a number of important and strong statements regarding education for the guidance of member countries. Where Indigenous peoples constitute a minority of the general population, nation states such as Australia, New Zealand, Canada and United States also have specific policy on education, health, housing and employment. Policy and report writing and formation does not appear to be the problem in making progress against racism, discrimination and social impediments, given that numerous policies and reports are available. The application of appropriate policy for diverse communities, policies that make a real difference is certainly problematic. This is mainly due to the clash of values, beliefs and cultures between dominant political and economic systems and their constituent communities and the extent of inequality that consequently exists across all aspects of society. In grappling with the problems of policy and the application of policy for Indigenous peoples, this book develops a realistic and integrated approach to schooling that takes as its centre point, Indigenous philosophy, learning and knowledge that exists in tension with dominant, non-Indigenous characteristics. At the same time, understandings and proposals for progressive educational change must be able to 'stand on their own two feet' within such tension and opposition, to respect and validate Indigenous culture and learning and by so-doing, strengthen education for all children. Each community needs to develop its own inclusive strategies for change and progress, demonstrating civic courage and persistence in striving for the public good and ultimately, human friendship and freedom.

Acknowledgements

We acknowledge the Elders, families and forebears of the Indigenous peoples of Australia and throughout the world. We recognise that the land on which we live, meet and learn is the place of age-old ceremonies of celebration, initiation and renewal and that the Indigenous people's living culture has a unique role in the history and life of us all (adapted from the Acknowledgement Policy, Victoria University Melbourne).

We acknowledge the support and solidarity of Indigenous communities in understanding what is possible for Indigenous education and the necessity of Indigenous and non-Indigenous people working together in democratic partnership for educational improvement and a more just society.

We acknowledge the collegial support of Dr Mauricette Hamilton. We thank her for reading and discussing our material and for making suggestions that enabled further thought and discussion. Through this process we were able to come to decisions that fashioned the final manuscript.

Finally, we acknowledge the support of reviewers and colleagues wherever they may be, who continue to work exhaustively for the recognition of Indigenous voice and aspiration, the view that we are one human species. It is extremely important in difficult times for progressive educators to know that they have the support of international practitioners, researchers, theorists and advocates in their united struggle against injustice and exclusion.

Figures and Tables

Figures

1	Organisational outline of chapters and main themes.	x
2	Organisational outline of chapters and main themes.	30
3	Internal and external language acts.	65
4	Philosophy of Citizen Education as social practice.	102

Tables

1	Worawa Way of living and learning.	28
2	Knowledge exemplar: Family.	37
3	Signature pedagogies of pragmatist application.	76
4	Summary features of neoliberal epistemology.	80
5	Principles of discursive learning.	87
6	Summary of key issues from Chapters 1, 3, 4, 5 and 6.	100

About the Authors

Neil Hooley
is an Honorary Fellow in the College of Arts and Education, Victoria University Melbourne and is an experienced academic and researcher. Within a pragmatist and inquiry paradigm, he has expertise with qualitative methodologies including narrative inquiry, case writing and case study and action research. His first book (*Narrative Life: Democratic Curriculum and Indigenous Learning*, Springer, 2009) proposes the incorporation of Indigenous culture and knowing into mainstream curriculum through the process of knowledge exemplars. His latest book (*Dialects of Knowing in Education*, Routledge, 2018) details an approach to knowledge production based on the dialectical theorising of practice and praxis and is an international contribution to the philosophy of education. Dr Hooley draws on Greek, European Enlightenment and American Pragmatism philosophies to understand knowledge, learning and schooling.

Lois Peeler
is Principal, Worawa Aboriginal College, Healesville, Victoria. Dr Peeler has spent many years in the state and federal public service, including with the Aboriginal and Torres Strait Islander Commission, advancing the cause of the Indigenous community and in particular, education. Worawa assists Aboriginal students to establish themselves in Australian society with a strong sense of Aboriginal identity and self-esteem. With hundreds of Aboriginal students attending from across Australia, many have overcome significant barriers to achieve their chosen goals. Worawa take immense pride in assisting students to reach their full potential. Emphasis is placed on threading culture through the curriculum and involving Aboriginal artists and other role models through a series of activities. The young women who pass through Worawa become strong and independent people, confident in their culture and Aboriginal identity and ready to take their place in the world.

Oksana Razoumova
is a lecturer with the College of Arts & Education, Victoria University Melbourne. As a linguist, she has had extensive teaching and research experience regarding the nature of language teaching and learning and its application in educational, employment and community settings. Dr Razoumova started her career as a Senior Lecturer at Minsk State Linguistic University in 1991 and moved to an educational management pathway after 3 years of her academic career. She worked as a Director of Studies in Auckland, New Zealand and Aca-

demic Manager ELICOS in Melbourne for nearly a decade. She developed a strong interest in leading language schools towards successful accreditation and re-accreditation, building professional teams of teachers with a particular research focus on professional and personal staff development.

Terminology

According to the United Nations, the term Indigenous refers to original peoples 'who inhabited a country or a geographical region at the time when people of different cultures or ethnic origins arrived. The new arrivals later became dominant through conquest, occupation, settlement or other means.' In addition, the term denotes peoples who have a direct and continuous relationship with the land, who accept self-identification as being Indigenous at the individual level and who are accepted by an Indigenous community as one of their members. Ancestral land has a fundamental importance for the collective physical and cultural survival of Indigenous peoples. They are also holders of unique languages, knowledge systems and beliefs and possess extensive knowledge of practices to sustain the natural environment. In this text, a capital letter is used for Indigenous people in the same way that a capital letter is used for English people, Russian people and the like. Grammar used in quotations is left unchanged. A capital letter is also used for the word Elder to denote respect and esteem. Other terms such as Aboriginal peoples, First Nations and Native peoples are also used in various locations of the world, depending on the political and cultural histories that exist.

CHAPTER 1

Global Trends and the Struggle for Indigeneity

> As long as poverty, injustice and gross inequality persist in our world, none of us can truly rest.
> NELSON MANDELA

∴

Over the past thirty years and more, social, economic and educational development for all people have occurred within global neoliberalism as developed within each country. Market rather than human imperatives generally dominate educational direction and purpose with explicit philosophy being markedly absent as a major driver. Neoliberal education is difficult to define in detail with curriculum and pedagogical application varying across systems. Such lack of definition however provides scope for innovative change and originality to meet local community need. This chapter discusses the concept and practice of Indigeneity in context of the modern world and briefly outlines the main features of neoliberalism as they impact on community, schooling and knowledge for Indigenous children. Good education is good education for all children.

1 What It Means to Be Indigenous

At the 2019 annual meeting of the United Nations Permanent Forum on Indigenous Issues, Chair Anne Nuorgam from Finland commented that 'Traditional knowledge is at the core of indigenous identity, culture and heritage around the world' and that 'it must be protected' (UN, 2019a). The Forum noted that 'Indigenous peoples make up less than six per cent of the world's population, but account for 15 per cent of the poorest on earth. They live in some 90 countries, represent 5,000 different cultures and speak the overwhelming majority of the world's estimated 6,700 languages.' Unfortunately, many such languages have become extinct and others who use colloquial speech on a daily basis have declining numbers. For these reasons, 2019 was declared by the United Nations as the International Year of Indigenous Languages. In order to have a realistic appreciation of these issues from an educational perspective, schools and education systems generally need to have a clear understanding of the term 'traditional knowledge' and the place of Indigenous knowledge in culture and language in contemporary societies and institutions. This is particularly important when Indigenous families and children are in the minority and must 'ride two horses at once' in coping with the requirements of the dominant society. These problems are compounded when the dominant society itself may not have an unambiguous and emphatic view of formal education, with the purpose and direction of different sectors being contested.

Formal education in its traditional form can be thought of as being primarily concerned with an accepted body of facts, ideas and procedures that are passed on to current generations of students. In contrast, progressive education (Dewey, 1963) places students in a dynamic relationship with knowledge, where they are encouraged to explore facts, ideas and procedures for themselves. Learning is conceived as an act of inquiry or doing by individuals and groups as they discuss and contrast what they think with classmates, friends and family (Wenger, 1998/2004).

Traditional and progressive approaches can be combined in various ways as participants converse with each other regarding the task or project at hand, while at the same time, bringing to bear their current understandings that have come from family and community experience. In many countries of the world, formal schooling has shifted from a more traditional to a more progressive approach to learning, especially in the major economies as the number of children in each class has decreased and has made activity and experiment feasible. This has been particularly the case in primary education, where the emphasis is on language development in the broad sense of the word (see Chapters 5 and 6) through play, painting, music, reading, discussion and the like, with personal knowledge emerging from experience. There has been a shift from instruction to construction. Formation of Indigenous culture and knowledge (Nakata, 2007, 2018) can be seen in a similar light.

Indigenous knowledge and western scientific knowledge while not being identical, have a close relationship. Both arise from observation and a desire to know (Archibald, Lee-Morgan, & De Santolo, 2019). Ideas are prompted from social activity, observation and discussion over time, processes that occur for all human knowledge around the world. Indigenous knowledge may be more local and be expressed in stories for interpretation, while science tends to generalise across locations and history and be often stated as somewhat abstract mathematical and scientific symbols and equations (Grayling, 2021). What is known as logical positivism in Western philosophy for example, demands that what is believed must be verified 'scientifically' or mathematically before acceptance, thereby denying a more humanistic, subjective or metaphysical view. With this outlook, Western science may seek 'objective' truth regarding the land, while Indigenous knowledge seeks a sustainable relationship with land and country. Methods may indeed be similar, but their objective is different. However, it is possible to recognise notions of story, legend and myth that infuse our understanding of knowledge from whatever origin and that assist how we think about experience. Family stories that we hear as children about the great storm of many years ago will connect our personal consciousness with what the teacher says about thunder, lightning and hail. Hughes, More and Williams (2004) summarises these tendencies when they suggest that Indigenous knowledge and ways of knowing involves learning from and deep listening to the land, proceeding from community interest, the respectful participation of Elders, holistic connections between knowledge, forms of observation and practical inquiry, longer time spans for consideration and the centrality of culture including language, ceremony and communication. It is possible to see similarity here with the idea of integrated knowledge and inquiry learning outlined by pragmatist philosophers and scholars and the basis of progressive education around the world (see Chapter 6). Indeed, it is one intention of this book, that all chapters respect Indigenous culture, language and knowledge and that approaches to understanding and learning as discussed bring together the key features of humanistic, cultural and scientific modes of acting and thinking in the interests of all peoples.

Learning from the land is a difficult concept for non-Indigenous people to grasp, but is at the heart of Indigeneity, or what it means to be Indigenous (Merlan, 2009). As a species we are all part of the universe, or of nature and therefore need to respect and take care of all the plants, animals, rocks and waters of earth. There is a united whole of existence, everything connected to everything else. Eagleton (2011, p. 230) puts this well when he comments that 'Body and world, subject and object, should exist in delicate equipoise, so that our environment is as expressive of human meanings as a language.' Many people around the world would increasingly agree with this sentiment, with large numbers taking action to conserve and protect the natural habitat and surroundings. (Pascoe's book, Dark Emu, referenced later, provides detail of the agricultural and environmental life of Indigenous Australians.) For Indigenous peoples, this relationship with the land is special, deeply felt, essential to who they are and how they have become who they are. Indigenous people live in different parts of the planet where the days may be cold and long, or humid and short, where the ground is covered with forest or sand, where the roar of the ocean is nearby, or rain falls sparingly, where there are stories of riding the whales, or of the flightless emu, where fish or the honey bees are plentiful. This closeness to the soil and its harvest and the seasons that change in harmony with the sun and moon, have forged over the centuries a kinship that integrates family and land in an unassailable bond that only those who have lived it, feel it, know it, deep within their consciousness of family and community.

2   Decolonising Education and Knowledge

For many countries of the world, including those that are former colonies, the schooling system and curriculum design are still essentially imperial and colonial in structure, where significant knowledge is decided by the state in the interests of the state and is packaged for distribution to students. As features of colonisation, where entire societies are dominated and manipulated by invading occupiers, where the colonised are sought to be assimilated into social and cultural practices of the dominant, these power relationships continue to exist for schools between staff and students, between students and knowledge and between personal learning and formal assessment. As one result, Indigenous languages and knowledges have been attacked and in all too many cases, eliminated. What is understood as the ideology of settler colonialism has not disappeared into the atmosphere. Within this context and depending on their economic and political conditions, Indigenous families may be in the position of deciding to send their children to a local school that follows the state, semi-colonial curriculum, or to a school that follows an Indigenous curriculum, if available. This decision may be made on the basis of whether economic or cultural outcomes are preferred, whether children are set on a pathway to qualification and socialisation through schooling as accepted by the dominant community, or a pathway to cultural immersion and independence as accepted by the Indigenous community. To adopt a philosophical stance towards appreciating this decision for families means confronting the question and tensions of whether Indigenous and non-Indigenous knowledge, learning and schooling can be reconciled.

'As a First Nations Swampy Cree woman, I am proud of my heritage,' so begins Priscilla Settee with her essay regarding Indigenous knowledges. She goes on to state (Settee, 2011, p. 445):

> I feel that we produce knowledges for both Indigenous peoples and others and not necessarily for their curiosity, but in the hope that such knowledges will make them better human beings and create the desperately required social change for Indigenous peoples and all peoples in a world that is increasingly becoming bereft of human values.

This is a statement of friendship and hope. Its humility is expressed in the modern world that must grapple with the development of ideas and social practices that have emerged from the boiling and seething cauldron of humanity. For example, in association with the development of the European Enlightenment and later, the Industrial Revolution, together with the establishment of modern science, issues of independent thinking for the citizenry, rationality rather than bias and superstition and progress towards certainty, were central. European philosophy at the time continued to grapple with centuries-old questions that remained to be resolved regarding what it means to be human, how to live well, how do we learn and know, where do notions of ethics and values come from and how do humans go about investigating knowledge. These are quandaries and explanations that are often expressed in the stories of Indigenous and non-Indigenous communities as a process of exploring meaning. Stories emerge over time regarding patterns in the night sky, the shape of hills and mountains, where do birds go in winter, why people become ill, where does kindness and cruelty come from. Thales, who is considered to be the first Greek philosopher around 585 BCE, proposed that water was the essential component of all things (Grayling, 2021, pp. 3–4). This can be seen as a logical conclusion from observing water everywhere in its various forms and being necessary for life. Another logical conclusion from the Greeks when observing that smoke rose in the air while the stone fell, was that the smoke and stone were finding their natural place. This story can certainly be accepted today as a logical concept for thinking about the movement of matter in space. Decolonising schooling and curriculum through reconciling Indigenous and non-Indigenous understandings does not destroy original stories and thinking, but builds on them, looks for connections, poses new questions and thinks anew about the complexities of social and physical worlds. This is the history of humankind.

3 Identity within Neoliberalism

In comparison to the concept of Indigeneity, the term identity is often used. The demand for recognition can be individual and group, not necessarily to be included in the broader society, but to be respected and accepted precisely for different qualities and customs. This can be difficult to achieve for multicultural communities where all citizens are expected to adhere to common laws and procedures, but at the same time continue to practise language and traditions from their home countries. In some respects, neoliberal economies should make the recognition of difference easier because of its emphasis on individual rights and personal freedoms. With attention on conservative values and political ideas neoliberalism can however exhibit internal contradictions with its stated aims making the exercise of difference problematic. It is worth quoting then at this stage the definition of neoliberalism by Harvey (2009, p. 2) to understand how this contradiction exists:

> Neoliberalism is in the first instance a theory of political economic practices that proposes that human well-being can best be advanced by liberating individual entrepreneurial freedoms and skills within an institutional framework characterised by strong property rights, free markets and free trade. The role of the state is to create and preserve an institutional framework appropriate to such practices. The state has to guarantee, for example, the quality and integrity of money. It must also set up those military, defence, police and legal structures and functions required to secure private property rights and to guarantee, by force if need be, the proper functioning of markets.

It can be difficult for all citizens to live with integrity under these circumstances, especially if the economic system is strongly market and profit driven. This is because the market will promote market interests, not necessarily the interests of society as a whole. Any modern economy is a complicated juggling act involving national and international features that, overall, can benefit some and disadvantage others. For his part, Milton Friedman as one of the economic and philosophical progenitors of neoliberalism, for which he won the Nobel Prize in 1976, was fully aware of the question of social inequality. He stressed that 'At the heart of the liberal philosophy is a belief in the dignity of the individual' and that as a result, the liberal 'will welcome measures that promote both freedom and equality – such as measures to eliminate monopoly power and to improve the operation of the market' (Friedman, 1962/2002, p. 195). Interestingly, he was in favour of private charity being used to alleviate poverty and, very reluctantly, state action against poverty that could provide a more effective way of achieving common community objectives. This demonstrates the contradiction between individual rights and freedoms on the one hand that impacts on the rights and freedoms of others on the other, whether this is intended or not. Inequality must be an outcome of neoliberal capitalism, where market opportunities for personal gain exist in fierce competition with the rights of others to do the same. It is not unusual that what is known as 'identity politics' has emerged over recent times, as neoliberalism has spread around the world. That is, the need to find expression and respect within economic systems that tend to submerge constituent groups in their wake.

The struggle for Indigenous identity and perhaps more significantly, Indigeneity, occurs within this often suffocating context. Consideration of the Dreaming is a case in point. For Indigenous peoples in Australia, the European word Dreaming denotes a coming together of personal and community being and strong intimate connections with the land and present-day conditions. The Dreaming is timeless, forever present. It is a state of mind, not to be confused with the images that might occur in the brain while asleep. It is consciousness or world view of existence rather than a religious view, as it does not involve the worship of gods or the following of a strict recorded code of doctrine and behaviour. An Aboriginal worldview presents an inviolable connection between people, the physical and spiritual worlds. All is connected from this perspective and relationship to the land is more than pivotal, it is ontological. This is described as 'ontological belonging' and this relationship constitutes the basis of Aboriginal identity In this respect, identity from the Dreaming is very much concerned with 'where I am from and who my family are.' There is a connection here with the scientific argument that since the beginning of European time and through the processes of evolution, the human race has originated from the earth, has occupied the earth, lives with the earth and returns to the earth. Stanner (1953/1979) noted the work of early Australian anthropologists, Spencer and Gillin (1899) when he discussed his non-Aboriginal understanding of The Dreaming as follows:

> The Australian Aborigines' outlook on the universe and man is shaped by a remarkable conception, which Spencer and Gillen immortalised as 'the dream time' or alcheringa of the Arunta or Aranda tribe. Comparable terms from other tribes are often almost untranslatable or mean literally something like 'men of old.' Some anthropologists have called it the Eternal Dream Time. I prefer to call it what many Aborigines call it in English: The Dreaming, or just, Dreaming. (p. 23)

As an esteemed anthropologist himself, Stanner goes on to link Aboriginal and non-Aboriginal philosophy and mutual ways of viewing the world. This insight, in combining the metaphysical and the material, relates closely to the integration of thinking and doing, or practice and theorising that underpins an accepted philosophical approach to knowledge production and indeed social life, today.

> In my own understanding, The Dreaming is a proof that the blackfellow shares with us two abilities which have largely made human history what it is. The first of these we might call 'the metaphysical gift.' I mean the

> ability to transcend oneself, to make acts of imagination so that one can stand 'outside' or 'away from' oneself, and turn the universe, oneself and one's fellows into objects of contemplation. The second ability is a 'drive' to try to 'make sense' out of human experience and to find some 'principle' in the whole human situation. This 'drive' is, in some way, built into the constitution of the human mind. No one who has real knowledge of Aboriginal life can have any doubt that they possess, and use, both abilities very much as we do. They differ from us only in the directions in which they turn their gifts, the idiom in which they express them, and the principles of intellectual control. (p. 32)

With this awareness, there is one human species that draws its identity, knowledge and understanding from the earth and subsequently is enabled to consider its place in the universe. It is difficult to define these fundamental contemplations exactly and perhaps this may not be necessary. Rather, we accept that there are different histories and cultures that inhabit the human sphere, all of which allow us to live, learn and love together.

4 Living between Worlds

Aboriginal Australian academic and journalist, Stan Grant describes below how he grapples with the question of his own identity (Grant, 2016, p. 174):

> I am often asked: What is an identity? It is a question that defies one convenient answer. Identity is forever in flux. Yet, there are those things that are essential to us: the permanence of family and the traditions of culture. Our history shapes us and, for my people, there is the legacy of racism. But Indigenous identity has been especially fraught, something inherently political. I shouldn't have to explain myself at all, but in Australia we have never had that privilege. It should be enough to say that I am a man of a Wiradjuri father and a Kamilaroi mother, a man who draws his ancestry too from white Australia. But my identity comes from navigating the space in between and having to explain that to an often uncompromising sceptical – even hostile – nation.

For many people around the world, 'the permanence of family and the traditions of culture' form the basis of identity (Langton, 2019). Growing up not only in a particular country, but in a particular place of country, seems to imprint upon the brain, whether in a big city or a small rural town, together with the people who are around us every day. We become a part of the language, history and customs of our community, feelings and understandings that lodge in our hearts and bind us together. For Indigenous peoples, 'navigating the space in between' multi-cultures can become a daily occurrence, often with ill-informed criticism and open aggression as accompaniments. Should it be necessary for identity to choose between separate black and white? Is it inevitable that we are locked into one view of seeing the world, to the detriment of others, generating hostility and hate? Will identity that has been composed at an earlier time and perhaps quickly remain dominant regardless of personal experience that accrues over a lifetime? Appreciating the structure of trees that we climbed as children, should allow us to wonder at the forest visage we travel through as adults elsewhere. Experiencing the freezing snow on a moonlight night brings back memories of winter at home. Asking for directions in a foreign land reminds us of stories told to us by grandma as we sat at her knee. Laughing and singing around the table or camp fire with newly-found friends when we don't know the words seem to be common around the world. Cultures are diverse, but there are many similarities that lay the basis for understanding and unity. In fact, trying to work through difference of family, home, language, history, land and nation is perhaps the single great task of humanity.

There is an argument that neoliberalism should lead to greater understanding between peoples and in the end, freedom. This is difficult to accept when we witness the existence of poverty, racism, war and aggression that continue year-by-year. However, poverty on a global scale is said to have reduced mainly because of the strength of the Chinese economy and the raising of living standards in that country. It is also suggested that the exchange of goods and services between people and countries does not depend on the race and background of those involved in production, but on the quality and necessity of the goods involved. Increased travel and access to communication technologies bring people closer together especially through major political, sporting and music events beamed world-wide. While these trends may be evident at the moment, there is still intense economic competition for markets and resources around the world that leads to constant political and military tension, always with the possibility of sparking antagonism and combativeness across borders. On the other hand, the concept of liberalism and the minimal role of government in the economy when coupled with capitalism leads to a laissez-faire situation of individuals making do as best they can, free to beg alms and sleep under bridges. Classical liberalism is concerned with liberty, civil and political, whereas modern liberalism (and neoliberalism) has adjusted to the nation state and the requirement to not only ensure individual rights, but to assist in areas such as health, education, poverty and housing. In the wealthier economies, neoliberalism against its better judgement, has had to develop state policies regarding many social welfare issues that were not present during an earlier time. As well as the development of capitalism, the struggle for national independence in colonial countries throughout the 20th century raised awareness of respect and dignity for all, rather than subjugation. The civil rights movement in the United States influenced many coloured and Indigenous peoples around the world to take action in support of claims for social justice and demands to take their rightful place in society. This particular struggle continues today with the 'Black Lives Matter' movement having international reach. What this means is that 'navigating between the space' is extremely complicated and arduous with the icebergs of capitalism, liberalism and neoliberalism for Indigenous and non-Indigenous communities alike affording dangerous flows at any one time. The fundamental differences between neoliberal thinking and indigenous peoples is the reification of the individual above the sense of community. While there is no doubt that individuals within indigenous communities have considerable agency, the very sense of being is determined by their intimate connections to place and space, to kin and community knowledge.

5   Sovereignty and Self-Determination

Quests for independence to enable the exercise of thought, action and dignity without coercion beat strongly in the breasts of justice-loving citizens and communities throughout the world. This is particularly the case for Indigenous populations where histories and cultures are often subjugated by hegemonic structures. However, according to the United Nations (UN, 2019b), 'Indigenous peoples have the right to self-determination. By virtue of that right, they freely determine their political status and freely pursue their economic, social and cultural development.' Within neoliberal economics and for all its deficiencies, it may be that representative democracy is one of the means of approaching this aspiration, where free and open elections establish legislatures that attempt to treat all fairly. It is difficult however for the few to accurately represent the views of the many, particularly in societies that are stratified by wealth and power. Devolving decision-making to smaller groups such as regions, villages and neighbourhoods can offer greater opportunity for participation of those directly impacted by the decisions. Within institutions, it should also be possible to ensure flatter arrangements of decision-making so that individuals and teams have authority for the conditions and outcomes of their work. There is a counter-side to the argument of minorities living within dominant societies, in that recognised and robust values and beliefs of the smaller group can often provide guidance for how current organisation and procedures can be changed for better overall results. For example, being highly respectful of the experience and views of Elders means that Indigenous communities have access to a corpus of history, culture and wisdom that can be prudently brought to bear on problems and issues as they occur. Institutions in all fields could adopt a similar approach, so that more experienced personnel are not overlooked, but have a valued role in mentoring and supporting other colleagues.

Self-determination as described by the United Nations above will be difficult to achieve, in fact, will be difficult to achieve for peoples everywhere. In the first instance, to 'freely determine their political status' can be taken to mean in each society principles such as equality under the law, non-discrimination regarding health, education, employment and the like, appropriate forms of taxation and expenditure and the right to live in accord with community customs and practices. Linked to these ideas is the right to 'freely pursue their economic, social and cultural development,' interpreted as the opportunity to engage in activities that enhance involvement with and understanding of the world for personal benefit, provided that these do not interfere with the rights of others to do so similarly. There are two pre-conditions that makes it extremely difficult for Indigenous peoples to be able to realise these principles. First, the existence of racism and colonialism that separates people on the basis of fear, uncertainty and political influence and second, severing relationship with land and language that makes continuity almost impossible. Somewhat tenuous connection between these two features of social life is shown by adoption of the Native Title Act in Australia in 1992. Title to land was granted when Indigenous nations could demonstrate continuous connection to country since British settlement in the 1770s and when title was not extinguished by the existence of previous acts of government. In 1996, the High Court of Australia clarified its initial decision by ruling that native title could coexist with pastoral leases under certain circumstances. This approach to Indigenous sovereignty and land ownership is still unsatisfactorily partial, complicated and unpredictable and specific cases may take many years to decide in the courts. Given the connections between land, culture and wealth around the world, the questions of self-determination for Indigenous communities will not be resolved until the powerful and supremacist show genuine respect for Indigenous land ownership and sharing of all natural and philosophical resources for public well-being.

6   Prospects for Indigenisation

It is unlikely that any dominant economic system of power and privilege will convert itself into its opposite without vigorous resistance. When contradictions exist however, it should be possible to identify and exploit points of weakness for social progress. Indigenous values for example are often at variance with capitalist economics, but in accord with the viewpoints of the majority population. In this regard, Pascoe (2014, p. 209) comments:

> One of the most fundamental differences between Aboriginal and non-Aboriginal people is the understanding of the relationship between people and land. Earth is the mother. Aboriginal people are born of the earth and individuals within the clan had responsibilities for particular streams, grasslands, trees, crops, animals and even seasons. The life of the clan was devoted to continuance.

Many people would claim an emotional closeness with the land, although the concept of 'Earth as mother' and being 'born of the earth' may not enter into that relationship, at least explicitly. It may be difficult to explain such intimacy with the physical environment, similar to many other instances where humans 'know what they experience and feel' but the words may not be adequate to confide with others. Family and community roots go deep. It may be difficult to explain clearly what it means to be Indigenous, British, Russian, Canadian or Egyptian to those who do not have Indigenous, British, Russian of Egyptian history, language and culture, but commonalities, events, key words and metaphors can be shared with respect and thoughtfulness. A particular approach to philosophy can be of assistance here. Before modern science became a distinct discipline during the European Enlightenment and the industrial revolution and distinguished itself from religion, the term 'natural philosophy' was used to denote studies of the natural word and the universe generally. To this day, natural philosophy considers a great unity where all objects of the universe are connected being made of similar material and functioning in accord with the general relationships that exist. What we currently understand as water for example has the same composition on other planets (when present) as it does in the human biological cell on Earth. When energy from our Sun travels through space as photons and enters our eyes allowing us to see externally, the same occurs for the eagle, lion and kangaroo. In this way, human consciousness, or awareness, or thought, is created, making connections between and within all that surrounds our being and continues to develop over time. Following Grant above, ideas, cultures and identities can be fluid and dynamic. We therefore envisage interrelatedness and correspondence between our notions of Indigeneity and natural philosophy.

Looking into recent history indicates that there has been a major contradiction during the industrial revolution period between respect for the environment and the provision of resources to support human development. The question of whether humans should exert sovereignty over the land, or whether we attempt to live in co-operation for mutual benefit, has caused ongoing concern. If all objects of the natural world are connected in some way, then the quest for ecological balance becomes an essential philosophical, historical and cultural problem. Considering the Earth as the basis of our existence demands the application of practice-theorising mentioned above. While the actual neurological processes that enable memory, emotion, knowledge, language and communication are still largely unknown, each person does interact with ocean, sky, clouds, rabbits, rivers and dew on the ground that form human intelligence, or how we interact with the world. Including, of course, community, friends and family, key aspects of the universe for us all. We construct a general approach to how things work, are integrated, connected and can be applied to other, quite different and novel situations, an approach to what is called consciousness. Described as the 'unresolved hard problem' of philosophy, Chalmers (2003) comments:

> The hard problem of consciousness is the problem of experience. Human beings have subjective experience: it is something it is like to be them. We can say that a being is conscious in this sense – or is phenomenally conscious as it is sometimes put – when there is something it is like to be that being. A mental state is conscious when there is something it is like to be in that state.

In this explanation from natural philosophy, human consciousness is seen as arising from social experience such that mental states in the brain are created whereby something is like something else. My family experience as a child, for example, generates feelings of love for country, brothers and sisters that becomes a part of my mental state and informs my awareness of like situations when they occur, when interacting with other people. A model of consciousness – perhaps in some respects, a model of what it means to be human – can be drafted in purely descriptive terms involving both metaphysical and empirical concepts without necessarily answering all questions or attempting to answer all questions completely and finally (Bronfenbrenner, 1979). Some might say that we should leave well alone and not pursue our quest for knowing and certainty too far and leave the detail of consciousness alone. As Chalmers opens his essay: 'Consciousness fits uneasily into our conception of the natural world.' However our discussion has taken us to the point where complex issues regarding humanity have emerged and it seems sensible to not put them aside. Within a general model of being then, the nature of experience as raised by Chalmers would suggest that it is social being that determines consciousness, not an isolated, individual consciousness that determines social being and capability. In this way, consciousness as a process of thought, of learning from experience and being aware of our own history, is universal to all humans, Indigenous and non-Indigenous alike. The evolutionary human species, sentient and cognitive, is responsive to all continuing social acts that constitute all cultural and communicative formations. Dialectical materialist consciousness based on the experience of land and society generates knowledge and learning for all of us, making the social and physical worlds accessible and knowable for everyone without discrimination.

7 Diversity and Harmony in Our Time

In reviewing the human journey thus far, we discern a series of trends within what might be called a highly contradictory admixture. On the one hand, history has not ended and it is clear that war, aggression, racism and inequality still dominate with apparently little prospect for their total elimination. On the other hand and speaking generally, there has been significant improvement in many areas of human endeavour including health, education, technologies and working conditions that contribute to increasing equity. Pinker (2018) for example, has argued that Enlightenment values of reason, science and humanism have brought inclinations towards prosperity, peace and indeed happiness compared with much earlier times. The dominance of neoliberal economics also exhibits internal contradictions, with its purest form sometimes exalted in policy terms, but often corrupted in practical application. Government spending and interference in market operation are decried, while at the same time, many programs demanded by the population need to be funded and administered. This trend has been emphasised by Piketty (2013, p. 571) when he comments:

> The overall conclusion of this study is that a market economy based on private property, if left to itself, contains powerful forces of convergence, associated in particular with the diffusion of knowledge and skills, but it also contains powerful forces of divergence which are potentially threatening to democratic societies and to the values of social justice on which they are based.

In his comprehensive work, Piketty is particularly concerned with equality and inequality within neoliberal capitalism. He proposes that the rate of return on capital and wealth accumulation grows at a faster rate than wages and income for working people, creating serious destabilising forces on market economies worldwide. This contrasts with a broadly accepted view of conventional economics, that inequality is low at low income levels, then increases as the economy strengthens, but decreases at very high income levels (Milanovic, 2016). That is, as the water level rises, all boats rise as well. On this basis in the more wealthy countries, inequality should be less with everyone benefiting from increased productivity and profit. Unfortunately this does not appear to be the case. Financial inequality that is a feature of the economic system will find its way into all other aspects of social life as well. Indigenous and non-Indigenous peoples therefore have a common interest in working together against inequality and for peace, justice and satisfaction. This is the quest for compassionate humanity. It involves delving deep into culture and sociality to grasp what is meaningful for all regardless of socio-economic background and dehumanising economics. Central characteristics of community, culture and language can be sought through systems of formal education, sanctioned by the state to achieve state interest, but allowing for creative minds to flourish with courage and commitment. Ways of knowing stretch across Indigenous and non-Indigenous consciousness and philosophy, similar and dissimilar but connected nevertheless. We can think about how to engage this prospect through the concept of polymath.

Indigeneity is a holistic state of mind, of being. Survival demands an intense and sympathetic knowledge of the environment, being able to adapt as the seasons change and food sources disappear or migrate. When one strategy is found to not be appropriate, another needs to be substituted. Some specialisation occurred as communities were formed and different tasks were assigned to different people. The Renaissance period in Europe covered the period between the 14th and 17th centuries and can be viewed as the transition to modernity as it is known today. Leonardo da Vinci is associated with this period and is considered to be perhaps the best known polymath. His talents extended across painting, mathematics, sculpture, anatomy, engineering and music. If we consider 'poly' as meaning more than one, or many and 'math' from the Greek: mathema, meaning that which is learnt, or what one gets to know, then we can agree with Ahmed (2018, pp. 2–3) that:

> Polymaths are multidimensional minds that pursue optimal performance and self-actualisation in its most complete rounded sense. Having such a mindset, they reject lifelong specialisation and instead tend to pursue various objectives that might seem disparate to the onlooker – simultaneously or in succession – via thought and/or action. The inimitable complexity of their minds and lives are what makes them uniquely human.

Such a view of a satisfying and fulfilled life, as much as it can be within the social and political conditions that exist, runs counter to the daily existence of most. However it remains a vision of aspiration that is attractive, albeit with one weakness – there is no reference to social purpose, of working and contributing for the good of community and general public. On the contrary, Indigenous Australian, David Unaipon (1872–1967), inventor, writer and lecturer made many contributions across a wide field of interest (Unaipon, 2020). It may not be necessary for every single person to have commitment to the public good and the role of the artisan, artist and polymath may have more specialised intent, perhaps of historical significance. It is certainly the case for instance, that Leonardo continues to inspire over a number of centuries, a wonderful example of art, mathematics, invention and beauty in combination, expressing in artefact profound human thought and knowledge. He epitomises what Ahmed suggests as the main categories for polymathy, those of individuality, curiosity, intelligence, versatility, creativity and unity (Ahmed, 2018, p. 116). David Unaipon who also embodied these categories demonstrates that Indigeneity is well-placed to take this tradition forward. Holistic identified lives, family and community-based, learning through land, observation, story and ceremony, guided by the wisdom of Elders and the stability of continuance over centuries, potentially at least, establishes spheres of harmony amidst the chaotic diversity and frenzy of modern living. A view of humans as being inherently community-oriented polymath rather than individual and specialist, not only links Indigenous and non-Indigenous being, but may be the philosophical trend or shift that is required to progress towards a more human ethical purpose and equilibrium.

In relation to the above discussion regarding global and historical contextual issues that impact on Indigenous education, Chapter 2 now describes in some detail a case study of Worawa Aboriginal College, Australia. Chapters 3 and 4 will then discuss key features arising from the Worawa program including the nature of knowledge and social practice, the philosophy of pragmatism and the significance of land and language for Indigenous education and learning generally. Based on these ideas, Chapter 5 proposes a broad and inclusive approach to education that respects the culture, knowledge and language of Indigenous and non-Indigenous children alike.

To frame discussion in forthcoming chapters, the 'Uluru Statement from the Heart' (Uluru, 2020; Reynolds, 2021) is reproduced in full below. Uluru is a sacred place in central Australia, a red/orange sandstone monolith formation that dominates what might be called the geological 'heart' of the country. The Uluru statement below expresses the aspirations of Indigenous peoples of Australia for recognition and respect. There is a request to be heard by the entire

Australian nation through the formal process of conversation and 'Voice,' to be enshrined in the Australian Constitution in the near future. In addition, there is a call to establish a process of 'Makarrata' for a 'fair and truthful relationship' with all the peoples of Australia. The 'Uluru Statement from the Heart' is a strategy for peace, justice and friendship and to correct the wrongs of racism and discrimination that have scared the dignity of history and humankind.

8 Uluru Statement from the Heart

We, gathered at the 2017 National Constitutional Convention, coming from all points of the southern sky, make this statement from the heart: Our Aboriginal and Torres Strait Islander tribes were the first sovereign Nations of the Australian continent and its adjacent islands, and possessed it under our own laws and customs. This our ancestors did, according to the reckoning of our culture, from the Creation, according to the common law from 'time immemorial,' and according to science more than 60,000 years ago.

This sovereignty is a spiritual notion: the ancestral tie between the land, or 'mother nature,' and the Aboriginal and Torres Strait Islander peoples who were born therefrom, remain attached thereto, and must one day return thither to be united with our ancestors. This link is the basis of the ownership of the soil, or better, of sovereignty. It has never been ceded or extinguished, and co-exists with the sovereignty of the Crown. How could it be otherwise?

That peoples possessed a land for sixty millennia and this sacred link disappears from world history in merely the last two hundred years? With substantive constitutional change and structural reform, we believe this ancient sovereignty can shine through as a fuller expression of Australia's nationhood.

Proportionally, we are the most incarcerated people on the planet. We are not an innately criminal people. Our children are alien ed from their families at unprecedented rates. This cannot be because we have no love for them. And our youth languish in detention in obscene numbers. They should be our hope for the future. These dimensions of our crisis tell plainly the structural nature of our problem. This is the torment of our powerlessness.

We seek constitutional reforms to empower our people and take a rightful place in our own country. When we have power over our destiny our children will flourish. They will walk in two worlds and their culture will be a gift to their country. We call for the establishment of a First Nations Voice enshrined in the Constitution.

Makarrata is the culmination of our agenda: the coming together after a struggle. It captures our aspirations for a fair and truthful relationship with the people of Australia and a better future for our children based on justice and self-determination. We seek a Makarrata Commission to supervise a process of agreement-making between governments and First Nations and truth-telling about our history. In 1967 we were counted, in 2017 we seek to be heard. We leave base camp and start our trek across this vast country. We invite you to walk with us in a movement of the Australian people for a better future.

9   Excursus 1: Sand and Sky

I had climbed these sand dunes many times before. Often, early in the morning before others had stirred and hopefully with only a gentle breeze for company. Nearing the top, it is possible to hear the surf growling and curling as it rushes towards the shore, finally dissipating energy at its outer limits. On reaching the summit, I gasp at the beauty that unfolds before me, never failing to impress. An immense skyscape of light blue fills my vision with a puff of white here and there. I am reminded that this is usually the only time I see this colour and its gentleness. Then, stretching as far as the eye can see to the left and right, a line that separates sky and sea, seemingly with a slight curve, but I have never known whether that is an illusion or not. This is perhaps the most beautiful sight I have ever seen and something that has always been there indelibly from my childhood. It is easy to understand that previous generations had wondered what was on the other side. Apparently beneath the horizon, the ocean heaves and swells with power and grace, mixing different hues of green, purple and violet. As they form and approach the shore, incessant waves sometimes produce caps of white, making threads of sharp contrast. My eye is drawn to the bottom of the dune, where a margin of golden sand greets the incoming water, as it has done since time began and will do forever. As a child, whether summer or winter, I would come here, to swim, run, sometimes fish from the pier, or just to sit and wonder at the combination of sight and sound that constantly changed. During winter, the cold south wind and sometimes driving rain would bite at my face and chill my bones, whipping the waves into fury as they crashed onto the sand. I marvelled at their strength and persistence. But I knew the seasons would alter, ultimately bringing the warmth of summer, barmy evenings and a sky of ink sprinkled with dots of brilliance. In many respects, I accept that these experiences have caused me to think the way I do, what I think is important for myself and others. Now, many years later, when I return and stand on those very same dunes of childhood, memories come flooding back, high tides of awareness and connection. This is my knowledge, my home.

CHAPTER 2

Case Study: Worawa Aboriginal College

> Aboriginal children must be educated in the way of our people. They must learn their history, about their great ancestors, the language and the law. It's time for them to know and understand themselves. They must also be educated in the ways of the society in which they live, in the very best of what it has to offer, so they can truly be part, not only of Australia's past, but also its present and future.
> PASTOR SIR DOUGLAS NICHOLLS (at the opening of Worawa, 1983)

∴

Worawa Aboriginal College in the state of Victoria, Australia, is a secondary college that combines Aboriginal culture and wellbeing with the recognised regular curriculum. It caters for Aboriginal girls in secondary schooling (Years 7–12) who come from urban, remote and very remote communities across Australia. After graduation from Worawa, students may choose to go on to higher education or return to their local communities to adopt community leadership roles. This chapter discusses key features of the Worawa experience and how these can inform and markedly change schooling of the neoliberal society. Considering the many contradictions and dialectic of Indigenous and non-Indigenous education and the connections and communication that links culture, discourse and meaning, establishes the context for Indigeneity to be a major aspect of mainstream schooling.

1 Living and Learning Together

On a mild and sunny day, the blue and purple of the surrounding hills merge with the nearby green, orange and brown of trees and foliage moving gently in the breeze. Occasionally, fog and mist will linger around hill-tops until mid-morning, before being replaced by bright light and blue skies. Situated 60 kilometres to the east of Melbourne on the former Coranderrk Aboriginal Station and near the picturesque township of Healesville in the tranquil Yarra Valley, Worawa Aboriginal College continues to honour the ideals of its founder, Aboriginal visionary Hyllus Maris. Speaking at the opening of the College in 1983, Hyllus said: '... in this, the first Aboriginal school in Victoria, the educational curriculum has been specially designed to suit Aboriginal students to bring them to their full potential. Aboriginal culture will be imparted not only as a school subject in each class's timetable but as an integral part of every-day life at the school.' The beautiful rolling hills and country setting of the college includes the world renowned Healesville Sanctuary specialising in native Australian animals and provides the opportunity for Worawa students to work alongside animal keepers as part of the Worawa ranger training program. Working at the Sanctuary enables students to interact with their totem and contemplate their relationship with the natural environment.

As described by Hamilton (2019) in her comprehensive study, Worawa Aboriginal College today is the only independent boarding school for Aboriginal girls in Australia and provides holistic education combining academic studies, culture and wellbeing. The college is owned and governed by Aboriginal people. The Worawa Model of Learning is grounded in Aboriginal values and ways of knowing, doing and being (see detailed description below). A council of Elders oversees the culture curriculum, while the Principal and Executive Director is Dr Lois Peeler AM, an Aboriginal woman of Yorta Yorta and Wurundjeri heritage. The academic program at Worawa is guided by the Australian Curriculum (ACARA, 2019) and is structured around a series of Learning Centres involving Aboriginal Culture, Health and Sport, Creative Arts, Languages, Mathematics and Science. The education program also includes personalised learning, digital portfolios, partnerships with other schools and organisations, vocational education experience, health, physical fitness and sport. In 2017 the College received approval from the Victorian Regulations and Qualifications Authority (VRQA) to adjust its educational delivery to include senior secondary years (11 & 12) and since 2018 has offered the Victorian Certificate of Applied Learning (VCAL/VCAA, 2020), recognised as satisfactory completion of secondary schooling.

Worawa recognises the importance of addressing health and wellbeing of students to enable them to focus on education. The college has consistently worked to evolve its wellbeing hub where research and evidence-based practices have led staff training to create a community of practice that can guide young Aboriginal women into their adult lives and beyond. A key focus of the College has been the co-design of the Worawa Model of Wellbeing. The college has a negotiated agreement with Monash Children's Hospital in Melbourne to have a paediatrics doctor visit the college two days per week. The college has a full time School Nurse, has service arrangements with external allied health services and has negotiated placement of a clinical psychologist one day per week. The appointment of a qualified social worker provides on-site assessment and counselling services to students as required. A student support worker assists students at times of 'Sorry Business,' bereavement when they have community 'worries' or need to connect with family.

2 Commitment to Education, Culture, Language and Wellbeing

The education program at Worawa has been designed to educate the whole person across all domains of their development, social, emotional, physical, spiritual, cultural and academic, acknowledging that '[e]very moment of life is a learning event, a creative participation in the complex choreography of existence' (Davis, Sumara, & Luce-Kapler, 2000, p. 178). The principal of the college therefore requires vision to plan and the ability to successfully implement such an education program. In providing learning opportunities and experiences that have personal meaning, Aunty Lois Peeler appreciates the implications for the trajectory of a learner's life, where learning opportunities and experiences are part of a holistic learning model. Based on lived experience, Aunty Lois understands the importance of a holistic approach to education, integrating academic development with health and wellbeing as well as culture, to develop an Aboriginal person, secure in her identity with the skills, ability and confidence to 'Walk in both Worlds.' The Worawa program is unique in the Indigenous Australian education landscape with evidence based practice developed over more than three decades of operation.

Each year the college conducts a School-Community Forum to engage the parents/families of students in their child's education and to hear from the families the aspirations they have for their child. The Elders are adamant that Aboriginal students need to develop the capacity to be 'two-way' learners. They need to learn from family and community and use this learning to help them learn within mainstream (Western/Scientific) culture. All students' parents are committed to two-way learning, where there is a strong cultural foundation. A number speak very emotionally about the changes in their young ones, since coming to Worawa; they value the girls learning more about and celebrating their own culture or where culture is already strong, they value their learning about the culture of others. They cite the ability to provide an education in a cultural context as the strength of Worawa, as they understand this will equip the girls to walk successfully in two worlds.

The School Community Forums enable the teaching staff to develop a personalised learning plan to meet the needs of each child and develop realistic pathways with the development of knowledge and skills that girls can take back to their community or to pursue higher education. Families participate in the college's Presentation Day held at the end of the school year to acknowledge and celebrate the achievements of students. A sense of community is enhanced through this and it is significant in that it ensures the development of structures that 'enable Indigenous families, children … to participate as respected equals in the learning process' (Hooley, 2009, p. 127).

Worawa Aboriginal College focuses on the education and wellbeing of Aboriginal girls and young women in the age range of 13 to 18 years. The specialist nature of Worawa's operations lie in its integrated model which combines personal development, intensive health and wellbeing programs with strong formal education principles and cultural activities led by Aboriginal Elders, focussing on Aboriginal values and pride in Aboriginal heritage.

3   Community-Based Expansion of Student Leadership Development Opportunities

Worawa conducts a Pathways to Womanhood program, a year-long capability and leadership development program of activities to support Aboriginal young women to make a healthy transition to adulthood. The Pathways to Womanhood program provides a pathway from developing personal care skills through to engaging in work experience, vocational activities and civic engagement. In this program the young women have the opportunity to enhance their personal and social development, develop a practice of healthy lifestyles and health-promoting behaviours focussing on self-care and personal presentation. The program requires the young women to cultivate cultural identity and gender awareness and culminates in a major social event called Debutante Dreaming, which involves partnerships with local schools, parents and members of the Worawa school community. This event encourages respectful relationships through social interaction with a partner school for boys who accompany Worawa students in the formal event. Public performances, in the presence of the Elders, are annual events. 'Debutante Dreaming' remembers the first Yorta Debutante Ball in 1949, and is a fusion of traditional Aboriginal ceremonial practice and Western tradition. The Pathways to Womanhood program therefore connects and empowers students in many ways. Being part of this program is a hallmark of students' immersion in their final year at Worawa. It carries many extra responsibilities in the boarding house and this involves personal and leadership responsibilities. Dinners are part of the program, where students socialise and speak publicly. The improvement in the ability of girls to speak publicly during their time at Worawa is noted by all members of the college community.

Aunty Lois is an Elder who has worked extensively in education and in the mainstream Australian world. Assisted by previous experience in government positions and a career in the performing arts and fashion, she demonstrates the ability to develop culturally appropriate learning experiences within the parameters of Australian and Victorian Government policy. This modelling is an essential aspect of rigorous two-way learning. It is evident that overall, Aunty Lois 'is someone who has the style, personal qualities, values, skills, experience and knowledge to 'mould consensus' and mobilise other people to get things done together' (see Indigenous Governance Toolkit, 2019). Accordingly and through their education at Worawa, students gain the confidence and ability to direct their own lives and continue their growth as strong, proud Aboriginal young women, who, whatever the future holds for them, can walk successfully in two worlds. Following are the words of self-assessment of two senior students when describing their appreciation of Worawa. By their words, they demonstrate that they are conscious of the change and development that has taken place as they were educated within a dynamic robust community adapting to changing circumstances:

> Worawa has shaped and transformed me from a scared immature girl to this grown up, confident and bright woman – a leader. (Worawa student, 2014)

> Worawa has changed my life it has given me an idea of where I want to go and what I want to do in the future. I don't know what I want to do but I feel confident. (Worawa student, 2014)

4 Culture Curriculum, Contemporary and Traditional

Outlined below is a series of curriculum features to illustrate this broad scope of the Worawa program, intended to strengthen cultural connections, intercultural understandings and intellectual diligence.

Australian Aboriginal culture is the oldest living culture on the planet, yet the teaching of Aboriginal culture and history is not compulsory in the Australian education system, creating a gap in mainstream education about Aboriginal culture, science, technology, history and achievement. However Aboriginal and Torres Strait Islander Histories and Culture is included in the Australian

Curriculum as what is termed a Cross Curriculum Priority. This means that there is flexibility for schools to incorporate this area in all subjects taking into account resources and other preferences (Peeler, 2021). For each Cross Curriculum Priority, a set of specific organising ideas reflects the essential knowledge, understandings and skills for that priority. The organising ideas are embedded in the content descriptions and elaborations of each learning area as appropriate. How these are incorporated into the curriculum is the responsibility of each school. The Victorian Curriculum and Assessment Authority provides advice on how to incorporate Aboriginal and Torres Strait Islander perspectives into each Learning Area. Worawa Aboriginal College through the strong cultural focus of its curriculum not only fulfils this recommendation but is able to provide materials and advice to other schools wishing to address this Cross Curriculum Priority in an appropriate manner.

Worawa Aboriginal College is located on land that once formed part of Coranderrk Aboriginal Station, a government operated Aboriginal Reserve. This site is of great cultural and historical significance to many Victorian Aboriginal families displaced by colonisation. Coranderrk Aboriginal Station was established in 1863, to provide land for the 'last of the Kulin' clans, custodians of traditional lands and forests east of Melbourne.

The Dreaming Trail is a cultural precinct within College grounds which support the cultural and wellbeing components of college life. The Dreaming Trail forms the basis of Aboriginal pedagogy and enables exploration and reinforcement of cultural and social values, traditional practice and history of Aboriginal people of Victoria contributing to the spiritual and cultural wellbeing of the Worawa community. It also serves to educate the broader community of the dispossession, dislocation and displacement of Aboriginal peoples from their traditional lands and the suppression of Aboriginal cultural ceremony, language, traditions, knowledge systems, social order and kinship systems, imposed government policies and the effect on contemporary Aboriginal peoples. Associated with the Dreaming Trail, the History Walk commemorates twenty-one Aboriginal leaders through a visual representation of memorial poles to recognise and honour their achievements. Individuals identified are acknowledged Change Makers and have been selected on the basis of their outstanding commitment to improving the position of Aboriginal people in Australian society.

Worawa Aboriginal College recognises both Western and Indigenous knowledge systems and perspectives and incorporates these into the curriculum, extra-curricular, cultural and community activities. The 'Worawa Cultural Connections' curriculum model visualises the central place of Aboriginal culture in each of the College's five Learning Centres, and the many cultural expressions. This model facilitates independent thinking and the development of research skills and creativity. Personalised instruction considers a student's prior learning and the pace at which she can progress. The importance of discipline/subject knowledge and expertise is foundational to the teacher's capacity to provide personalised learning, consisting of learning activities which are tailored to the needs of each individual student and are designed to challenge and extend student's knowledge, skills and understandings. This is congruent with Vygotsky's (1973) Zone of Proximal Development.

The Worawa curriculum incorporates rich heritage expressed through narrative, song, dance and visual artistic expression from both contemporary and traditional perspectives. As well as traditional and contemporary arts practices, personal and community narratives, the curriculum also includes new perspectives and expressions of identity, stories, history, and experiences of contemporary Aboriginal Australia. The teaching of Aboriginal culture and history is fundamental to this purpose and an essential component of the College's integrated academic, culture and wellbeing model. Aboriginal Studies are part of the total and on-going curriculum. The Worawa Culture Program has been designed to foster student knowledge, understanding and appreciation of the diversity of Aboriginal Australia's culture and history.

4.1   Media Arts

The need to incorporate Media Arts into the curriculum has been identified to ensure students have access to many art forms that will support a positive effect on their ability to create and express themselves. The Australian Curriculum states that the inclusion of Media Arts involves creating representations of the world and telling stories through communication technologies such as television, film, video, newspapers, radio, video games, the internet and mobile media. The Media Arts program involves students learning to engage with communication technologies and cross-disciplinary art forms to design, produce, distribute and interact with a range of print, audio, screen-based or hybrid artworks. As curriculum projects, each year students are involved in the production of the college year book and also undertake collection of community oral histories.

4.2   Polytechnic

Worawa Aboriginal College has a climate-controlled greenhouse established specifically for the propagation of native plants for food and botanicals. Activities include propagation of the Aboriginal staple food plant, Murnong or Yam Daisy. The project has sparked interest with the Commonwealth Scientific and Industrial Research Organisation (CSIRO), universities and local business operators. The project integrates bush food production into the college curriculum and student learning activities to develop student interest and knowledge to transition to careers/employment within the native food and botanicals industries.

4.3 Cadet Rangers

The Worawa Cadet Ranger Program is based upon three integrated activity areas that combine basic natural and cultural resource management with outdoor recreation. The natural and cultural resource management activity areas are designed to expose participants to activities and personal development associated with:

- Identification of basic environmental and cultural elements within the landscape.
- Understanding processes that lead to the presence and current state of basic environmental and cultural elements.
- Assessment of the current state and potential impacts upon basic cultural and environmental elements within the landscape
- Mitigation of negative impacts upon basic cultural and environmental elements within the landscape.

These four foundation processes may be applied to any individual cultural or natural heritage elements or group of elements and correspond with a progressive four-part learning structure associated with the program. Within this learning structure, Worawa Cadet Rangers undertake training in the classroom, in environmental settings and within workplace placements.

4.4 STEAM

In accord with encouraging student engagement with science, technology, engineering, arts and mathematics (STEAM) programs, students are able to express their innovation and creativity with a range of exciting projects focusing on wearables and electronics. Worawa has a number of industry partnerships that ensures that girls have the opportunity to experience genuine workplace scenarios in the merging of cutting edge and traditional technologies. An example is the college partnership with the local Yarra Ranges Tech School which enables students to experience working in design teams using the latest technology with an electronics basis and in a real-world context. This process eventuated in students coming up with a range of advanced wearable technologies to measure heart rate, footsteps and body temperature as well as a portable Bluetooth-enabled surround sound system.

A partnership with the CSIRO focuses on climate change, the Worawa weather station and experiencing the function of solar energy. This project includes an excursion to see the experimental lightweight and flexible solar film in action at a trial installation at Melbourne Zoo. Resulting from this project, students are working with CSIRO to create an installation incorporating solar lighting on the memorial to the Children of Coranderrk on the college's Dreaming Trail. The University of Melbourne and the Bureau of Meteorology (BOM) work with students in areas of science and technology in relation to Indigenous seasonal calendars based on observing the weather conditions and changes in nature. The BOM use the data generated from the Worawa Weather Station as part of a national program monitoring weather patterns and conditions. The University of Melbourne School of Computing and Information Systems work with students in a number of projects which includes gene technology and the use of computer programs to manoeuvre drones.

College programs in Mathematics, Science/Environment, Health and PE and The Arts are academically based, enriched with extra-curricular activities and cultural overlays and strengthened by a range of partnerships in the academic, sports, health and creative arts sectors. An annual calendar incorporating creative/performing arts, sport and cultural presentations and events is developed in consultation and coordination with all members of the college community. Literacy and English language development and proficiency is therefore integrated across the curriculum so that oral and written expression are directly related to experience and communication.

4.5 Arts

At Worawa the arts program is a means by which narratives can be told and developed through dance, music and visual arts, reflecting stories of community, family and land. The arts generally enable rich Aboriginal history and culture to be expressed through a wide range of personal and community expression from both traditional and contemporary perspectives. Using the ancient traditions of narrative and the arts, students are encouraged to relate the methods of the Ancestors in transmission of culture through the oral tradition, such as yarning (informal talking), song and dance, thus empowering them through honouring their stories and histories. In both the visual and performing arts curriculum, students are encouraged to express themselves and to share and explore their own cultural knowledge, while attempting new and challenging forms. A partnership with the Australian Chamber Orchestra – Inspire introduced students to orchestral music and instruments. The College has an association with Aboriginal Opera Singer Deborah Cheetham and Short Black Opera and a developing partnership with the Australian Girls' Choir. In this way, students have constant exposure to a range of traditional Aboriginal art styles through established traditional artists in their family and Aboriginal communities from many parts of Australia who tell their Dreaming and personal stories through art.

> I paint the world black and the design white. A big barramundi with a big city inside. Melbourne city. A big water hole, in the middle, where I was born. It reaches to each corner. In colours just black and white, I weave through my story. I paint this world with dots, waterholes and circles inside of circles getting smaller and smaller, with wavy lines, all white. (Justine, Worawa Aboriginal College student, September 2019)

5 Curriculum, a Holistic Experience

An explicit philosophy of education underpins the approach taken towards learning and curriculum at Worawa. Rigorous learning at the college has a particular meaning and includes pedagogical approaches that encourage cultural, critical and creative learning, structured personalised learning and high expectations in keeping with mainstream educational anticipations. Learning is understood as being bicultural and give particular attention to Indigenous-focused pedagogies, with particular respect to knowledge illuminating Aboriginal Ways of Knowing, Doing and Being. These reflect the communal and relational nature of Indigenous knowledges that connect individuals with family and kin, country, culture and spirituality. Knowledges are place-based or context-focused more than content-orientated. Working from the familiar to the less familiar or more abstract is an effective way of developing and 'chunking' learning for more efficient knowledge and skills acquisition. In total, these principles are described as 'The Worawa Way' and involves the fusion of Indigenous and non-Indigenous knowledge philosophies (Table 1).

TABLE 1 Worawa Way of living and learning

Relationship Ways of Being	Responsibility Ways of Knowing	Rigour Ways of Doing	Respect Ways of Valuing
Discussion-based Learning Collaborative learning Socially supportive Holistic learning	Individual learning Independent learning Discovery learning Observation-based learning	Creative, adaptive learning Hands-on learning Problem-based learning Scaffolded learning	Connected learning Narrative-based learning Place-based learning Cultural, value-based learning

Strong links can be drawn between these key features of learning and knowledge and the notion of 'discursiveness' discussed in Chapter 4. That is, a language-abundant environment that surrounds student action, discussion, reflection and intellectual risk. Language here has a broad definition of empowerment regarding the series of social acts that characterise human life across country and community forming the basis of holistic and integrated knowledge, immediate and abstract. While Table 1 lists a number of various approaches to teaching and learning, there is a close similarity or connectedness between them in that all are practice-oriented drawing on personal, cultural and historical backgrounds. Rather than being top-down or imposed, knowledge is built from experience, within the respect, discipline and context of community understandings, but arising from individual thought nevertheless. In discussing the notion of 'both-ways' (or 'two-way,' Hooley, 2009) education and learning, van Gelderen and Guthadjaka (2019, p. 5) note how the northern Australian Aboriginal community Warramiri, incorporate different world views while at the same time, not being submerged by outside influences:

> In one sense, it is unnecessary to link Warramiri philosophising with broader academic categories or theories; 'Bothways,' by definition, represents the legitimacy and power of different theories and epistemologies working together, whilst retaining their distinctiveness. However, 'Bothways' also represents the position that in the process of negotiating knowledge practices, new ideas and indeed, worlds are born; 'in this Yolŋu metaphysics, the knowable world comes out of the action, not the other way around.' (Christie, 2013, p. 52)

In commenting that 'the knowable world comes out of action,' Christie links Indigenous Yolngu (northern Australia Indigenous community) and non-Indigenous philosophy through in particular, pragmatism, practice and praxis, not for one perspective to dominate the other, but as equals in knowledge production. Consequently, it is possible to also explore a matrix of philosophical relationships regarding the 'Worawa Way' (Figure 2).

It can be seen here that 'Ways of Being' (Relationship) correlate with ontological understandings of what it means to be human, of thinking about the concept of 'human nature' and of 'species being,' the differences between human and other life and non-life forms on earth and beyond. It is generally taken that Indigenous philosophy conceives of everything connected to everything else and hence the need to respect all features of the environment. Naturalist philosophy has a similar view. Epistemology connects with 'Ways of Knowing' (Responsibility) whereby humans construct their own understandings and knowledges of the world through their participation with it, over

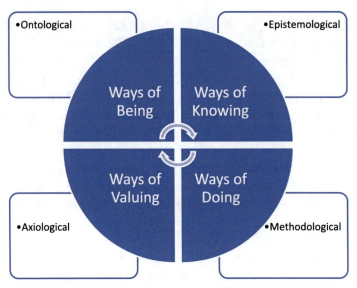

FIGURE 2   Organisational outline of chapters and main themes

time. As shown above (Table 1), human knowledge has the characteristics of 'meaning and purpose' as distinct from haphazard and disconnected data and information. In this sense, continuity of understanding is therefore significant for Indigenous and non-Indigenous philosophy and is established through story and narrative of various types, formal and informal. Knowledge protocols exist as 'Ways of Doing' (Rigour) within accepted methodological practices. Such practices may be peculiar to different communities, but draw upon commonalities such as the role of Elders, observations of experience and previous projects. Approaches to knowledge generally sit within broader frameworks or paradigms of understanding that provide continuity, although changes are possible when contradictory results occur. Finally, 'Ways of Valuing' (Respect) generate notions of axiology concerning ethical conduct and aesthetic belief. It is common in different cultures to have views of what ought be done generally and preferred actions under specific conditions and accordingly, to have shared understandings of what is satisfying and indeed, beautiful. Living ethically with others in peaceful or difficult times, in non-discriminatory and non-exclusionary terms, is certainly a means of constructing human fulfillment.

> I call out to this mountain valley, am I strong? The eagle and the mountains and the flowers and the ground and the leaves and the wind listen. Am I strong? They say nothing. But they're listening. (Rose, Worawa Aboriginal College student, September 2019)

In considering the 'Worawa Way' as a respectful meeting of Indigenous and non-Indigenous philosophies provides holistic strategies for opening up knowledge and learning for all peoples and a progressive basis for the school curriculum.

6   Bringing Peoples and Ideas Together

Development and application of the 'Worawa Way' is a serious attempt at strengthening Indigenous education, culture and wellbeing so that graduates can move as easily as possible between their different lives, responsibilities and communities. There are difficulties of course regarding the employment of appropriate staff who are able to stay for a considerable length of time, the constant development of curriculum not only in cultural terms, but in relation to ideological schooling systems as well, the provision of resources including digital technologies, the formation of partnerships with a range of different school and community organisations to broaden experiences and, inevitably, the clear demonstration of academic outcomes for external scrutiny. These difficulties must be confronted within the context of different languages, mythologies, customs and sciences of different histories and cultures resident with different peoples. For example, Andrews (2019, p. 17) comments on how the concept of 'law' is understood within Indigenous Australian society:

> As the Dreamtime Ancestors moved throughout the land, creating and naming everything, they laid down creation laws that are firmly fixed and immoveable. These are not so much 'laws' in the legal sense of case law, legislation and precedent. They are more in tune with Natural Law, a body of unchanging moral principles doing two things. Regulating human conduct in one sense and as observable law relating to natural phenomena in another. It is in both senses, that Aboriginal people refer to as 'the Law.'

Andrews goes on to discuss the difference between 'law' and 'lore,' meaning in the latter case, the notion of 'culture' that is passed on from generation to generation. In contrast, she defines 'law' as 'society's rules and regulations governing human behaviour ... the rights and wrongs of culture' (p. 18). This is a significant distinction that will often cause friction between procedures of Indigenous and non-Indigenous communities – and no doubt, friction within dominant schooling systems. Article 14.1 of the United Nations Declaration on the Rights of Indigenous Peoples (UN, 2007) is unequivocal in dealing with this problem in stating that, 'Indigenous peoples have the right to establish and control their education systems and institutions providing education in their own languages, in a manner appropriate to their cultural methods of teaching and learning.' Without a comprehensive understanding of philosophy, especially one that respects the connections between the natural and social worlds and enables different practices to co-exist as the basis of knowledge construction, then educational prospects for thinking the known and the unknown, the possible and impossible, as the basis of any curriculum, are remote.

From the discussion thus far, it can be summarised that the international Indigenous project of modernity and the quest for cultural definition needs to establish the authority and credentials of an Indigenous philosophy and epistemology if the different cultures of the world are to develop in non-racist ways and share and reconcile with each other. It is certainly a necessity for Indigenous peoples who wish to participate in dominate non-Indigenous forms of schooling. There are significant decisions and compromises that need to be made by competing viewpoints in support of the general philosophies that underscore progressive and neoliberal approaches to education. The claim for an explicit and emphatic Indigenous philosophy is not an assimilationist proposal to accept conservative European analysis and to assuage difference, but the opposite, to search for a set of precepts that seek to explicate human understanding to the greatest extent within a unified humanity.

7 Indigenous Knowledge as Cultural Practice

Human culture, knowledge and language are central aspects in the struggle for survival and meaning. All relate to what it means to be human and the evolution of consciousness that relates what we know to our continuing experience and philosophical investigation of what we do not know. Culture for example is a broad concept encompassing many ideas and can be difficult to define. The British writer T. S. Eliot (1948, p. 120) made the following observation:

> By 'culture' then, I mean first of all what the anthropologists mean, the way of life of a particular people living together in one place. Their culture is made visible in their arts, in their social systems, in their habits and customs, in their religion. But these things added together do not constitute the culture, though we often speak for convenience as if they did. These things are simply the parts into which a culture can be atomised, as a human body can.

In describing culture as 'the way of life of a particular people living together in one place,' Eliot suggests subjective feelings of togetherness or connectedness that arise from the general sweep of social practice, the good times and the difficult, throughout history. These feelings are in addition to participation in the actual social acts of say ceremony, music, painting, story and family and community interactions, the 'forms of associated living' mentioned by Dewey. Our relationship with the land and country comes about by our participation and learning with all its features that generates personal attachment and affection with the natural world. Intimate knowledge of river, flower and eagle will have similar effects. As noted in Chapter 1, Indigenous knowledge and ways of knowing are central concerns of Indigenous culture and fit nicely with the view of Eliot. That is, we can envisage Indigenous culture as the 'habits and customs' that involve learning from the land, proceeding from community interest, the respectful participation of Elders, holistic connections between knowledge, forms of observation and practical inquiry, longer time spans for consideration and the centrality of language, ceremony and communication. Looked at in this way, culture is social practice, or thought in action, in all societies and provides many bridges of understanding between diverse experience and aspiration.

Indigenous culture and knowledge may be difficult for non-Indigenous people to understand and appreciate. The reverse may also be true. Native Canadian writer Battiste (2015, p. 33) adopts an uncompromising attitude towards this tension when she draws a connection between culture and education and comments on the need for an approach to education that accepts:

> ... first and foremost, cognitive imperialism and its multiple strategies and replaces it with reconciliation through affirmation of the diverse heritages, consciousnesses and languages of Aboriginal peoples. The next measure is for a trans-systemic evaluation of both Indigenous knowledges and euro-Canadian knowledges and how they can be framed for curriculum, systems and training.

Battiste clearly identifies dominant economies in neoliberal countries as pursuing 'cognitive imperialism' through regular schooling, even though within that, there is ongoing conflict with minority cultures and minorities for survival. She argues that the way forward is to bring different knowledges together so that more appropriate curriculum formats can be devised. It is important to note that reconciliation notions of 'inclusion' and 'equity' should not refer to mere cosmetic changes of mainstream curriculum with the addition of some Indigenous content, but should result in curriculum of a different philosophical type, that welcomes diverse backgrounds and understandings respectfully and equitably. If ceremony is a central principle of culture and learning, then ceremony needs to be incorporated across the curriculum for all children such that patterns, words and objects are involved. Celebrations of progress in school mathematics and science can emphasise projects that have investigated the land and its protection. Compositions in music and dance can highlight how we cope with delight and sadness. Writing letters to family members near and far can demonstrate the significance of history and continuity. These events are common to different cultures and infuse not only our construction of knowledge, but our sense of place and community. While there are many positive attributes of this approach, the dispossession of ancestral land makes the recognition of Indigenous culture for education problematic and requires that all peoples of a region work together with good will and moral purpose to analyse what is common and valued. A strong critique of neoliberal economics and education is therefore the essential starting point.

As noted above, much dedicated work has been done by progressive educators around the world to respect and recognise Indigenous culture and knowledge as key aspects of regular curriculum and education generally (Cajete, 2019). In discussing the work of Jane Addams, Seigfried (2002, p. xviii) also reminds us that Addams highly valued social experience, involving the 'insatiable curiosity of children' and that 'For pragmatists, experience does not mean a private inner life, but a transactive process that encompasses self and world.' This describes the dialectical process between what we think and what we do, particularly in the company of others, where our projects of problem-posing and problem-solving cannot but expose our inner-most thoughts and guide subsequent actions arising. Working together on a piece of music to narrate the conclusion of a sporting season, or planning a school play for parents and friends, must involve the sharing of hopes and anticipations, of reaching deep down into what we think. Children of all ages and cultures do indeed reveal their 'insatiable curiosity' and energy for learning, a characteristic that can be extended to include all peoples since time began. This understanding does not assuage cultural difference, or attempt to assimilate one culture into another, but it does acknowledge commonalities regarding how humans go about engaging with their environments and the practices that are developed for survival, change and improvement. Recognition of both commonality and difference is the basis for a more just and harmonious society, but advocating that neoliberal education systems accept approaches to teaching, learning and curriculum that are pluralist including a range of cultural and world views is a substantial challenge. A closer epistemological definition of key aspects of experience, language and culture is therefore necessary.

8   Knowledge Exemplars – Two-way Inquiry Learning

Dewey saw education as a philosophical and democratic endeavour that could bridge the divide between nature and culture if conducted in an inquiry manner. He saw progressive schooling as a form of social life from which interest in learning from all the encounters of life establishes the essential moral interest. Attempting to bring together and learn from different cultures including the Indigenous and non-Indigenous is a moral and historical undertaking to be approached with commitment and courage.

Significantly then, regarding the nature/culture dialectic and in her continuing discussion of Worawa Aboriginal College, Hamilton (op cit) makes a summary statement that the college operates within a two-way cultural model, where Aboriginal culture and mainstream Australian culture combine in 'The Worawa Way.' This is congruent with a pedagogical design appropriate for Indigenous students, as learning is framed according to Aboriginal and mainstream Australian cultural constructs. 'Two-way inquiry learning' (Hooley, 2009) is an epistemological approach based on Dewey's approach to inquiry and learning which is dynamic in that it is concerned with the continuing understanding of life as experienced by real people and therefore has social and community connections. At Worawa, all sectors of the Aboriginal community are involved in the operation of the college. Reflection is part of their ongoing involvement, holistic, linked to the land and the real lives of students and personalised for each. Learning from both cultures Aboriginal and mainstream Australian, combine to form the basis of new understandings. This design ensures cultural inclusivity as both Indigenous and non-Indigenous epistemologies are integral to the learning and neither is understood as superior or inferior. Rigour is ensured through the involvement of the Aboriginal community in the Aboriginal cultural elements of the curriculum and through the use of the ACARA Australian Curriculum to frame mainstream curriculum. These two foci do not operate discretely, as the cultural elements provide two-way connections with the regular curriculum. The Elders, parents and grandparents through their interest in and suggestions for student learning, exhibit an organic relationship with the college. Through this, knowledge from mainstream curriculum and Aboriginal knowledges combine in a rigorous relevant learning program. Truth rather than being the property of a single culture is then recognised as multi-faceted and develops through robust discussion of different viewpoints within a democratic scenario.

> It's like you're holding something really old. When you carry the language, you're carrying the land and you're carrying the people with you. No matter where you go. No matter how much time goes by, it's still going to be there, inside of us. Nobody knows what's inside of us, but us. (Mary, Worawa Aboriginal College student, September 2019)

The two-way model acknowledges the contact zone (Sarra, 2011) demonstrating the understanding that Aboriginal people function in a position bounded at the extremes by an Aboriginal worldview and a western scientific worldview. Aboriginal Australian educator and musician Mandawuy Yunupingu (1999) in recalling his 'experience of becoming an educated, literate person, in and across two cultures, Yolngu and Balanda,' refers to this skill as '"double power," the power to operate in and negotiate between two cultures' (p. 1). He speaks of the fusion of the two cultures, not to oppose each other but to work together. As a younger person he realised that Aboriginal people had to acknowledge Western ideas and accept the positive and reject the negative. Achieving this would enable Aboriginal people to maintain control of their destiny. Models of schooling such as that at Worawa enable the continued pursuit of an Aboriginal ontology and epistemology.

Application of the above principles in curriculum and teaching for Indigenous children that is based on participatory inquiry learning and integrated knowledge is not an easy task at Worawa or at other schools. A practice/praxis way of thinking about this problem is through the concept of 'knowledge exemplars,' based on negotiated projects of student interest and the compilation of student portfolios as investigations proceed. Portfolios consist of various artefacts regarding the project such as photographs, interviews, newspaper articles, diary notes, internet resources and the like and provide the basis for group discussion, description and reflection. They need to show links with local history, culture and language and document engagement with important ideas. A sample knowledge exemplar suggested by Hooley (2009, p. 198) outlines an investigation of family characteristics and interests.

As collaborative small groups or learning circles of students work on their project and portfolios are compiled, a broadly-based knowledge exemplar is constructed. This can take the form of a single discussion document including the features noted in Table 2, together with appropriate artefacts selected to demonstrate important ideas arising from the overall investigation.

Making public the results of the project could involve community meetings with parents and Elders where students discuss and reflect upon their learning journey, where correlations with regular curriculum content can be made and where Elders can provide suggestions and validation for the work undertaken. In this way, a number of knowledge exemplars will be produced over time and will become available for different groups of students at different year levels to consider and extend through their own investigation. A curriculum consisting of knowledge exemplars based on student and community experience can include specific Indigenous and non-Indigenous content workshops to pursue ideas and problems that arise in the normal process of student curiosity and desire to know. Dewey's recommendation for freedom of inquiry to 'create intellectual and moral integration out of present disordered conditions' could

CASE STUDY: WORAWA ABORIGINAL COLLEGE

TABLE 2 Knowledge exemplar: Family

Knowledge exemplar features	Indicator 1 Family and country	Indicator 2 Importance of family	Indicator 3 Community events	Indicator 4 Work experience
Community	Connection with country	Kinship	Health	Survival, meaning
Community culture	Story by Elders	Story by Elders	Community wellbeing	Sharing resources
Artefacts	Newspaper articles	Photographs	Interview on computer	Implements used
Ideas, knowledge	Place of rivers in country	Influence of family members	Indigenous food	Interaction with broad community
Curriculum	Local history and geography	Community histories	Science	Industrial history
Reflection	Discussion with Elders	Views of community	Interviews with nurses	Interviews with employers
Making public	Parent-teacher nights	School displays	Feature article in newspapers	Employer newsletters
Curriculum implications	Ensure projects involve family, community	Suitable for history, geography, science	Literacy, numeracy, ICT	Key ideas, family timelines, droughts, employment

well be undertaken in the education field through imaginative combinations of the 'Worawa Way,' portfolios, knowledge exemplars and commitment to peace and justice.

9 Excursus 2: Indigenous Science, or Not

One of the issues that first struck me when reading about Indigenous education in various places around the world, was the close connections with notions of social practice and learning by doing. I was excited by this, as it provided more avenues for progressive curriculum change at my school, especially as a mathematics and science teacher. It was difficult for me to explicitly implement 'Indigenous ways of knowing' in my classes due to the small number of Indigenous children involved in a large suburban secondary school, but I was encouraged by the similarity of viewpoint between myself and Indigenous brothers and sisters elsewhere. I then became aware of trends towards the development of national curriculum, not only in Australia but in a number of other countries. Various attempts had been made over previous years, but reaching consensus across diverse political and educational stake holders was proving almost impossible. Believing I had nothing to lose, I managed to arrange for an interview with a senior educational bureaucrat who had a key role in conceptual development of the national curriculum and I knew had expressed what I took to be a reasonable view of knowledge production. During our discussion, I handed over some written suggestions regarding Indigenous education and the names of some respected Elders who might be involved on an advisory group. As time went by and organisation of the national curriculum proceeded in a very public, complicated and often contentious manner, I happened to hear my senior bureaucrat giving a radio interview, in which he very firmly stated that 'Indigenous science' would not be a part of the science curriculum! I was surprised and disappointed by this, as I saw the many connections between Indigenous ways of knowing and relationship with the natural environment having very much a science base. It seemed clear that this decision to exclude Indigenous observation, thinking and practice was a political and not an educational view. Some years later, understanding within the profession had moved on and today, there is an impressive list of accepted Indigenous 'illustrations' or suggestions available for the national curriculum for all students that show exactly that, detailed relationship with the land, plants and animals that link Indigenous and non-Indigenous thinking and reflection. Much non-Indigenous science has originated throughout the centuries in this way as we look at the sky, collect the honey of bees, consider the flight of birds and explore the deepest seas and highest mountains. Slow motion video cameras have opened up the wonder of the natural world to millions of people worldwide. We cannot not think, wonder and theorise. It seems appropriate that Indigenous and non-Indigenous friends should sit around the camp fire and share their integrated scientific thoughts and experiences for a deeper understanding of what is and what might be.

CHAPTER 3

Experience through the Arts

> As an artist I come to sing, but as a citizen, I will always speak for peace and no-one can silence me in this.
> PAUL ROBESON

∴

While social life provides the basis for human satisfaction and contentment, there is need for the continuing expression of thought and imagination in a range of forms that push beyond current practices. Social life embodies the meaningful and beautiful, but these aspects of existence can be further extended and taken to a higher plane of understanding such that the universals of everyday life become more acute, more vivid, more accessible and more personal than previously grasped. This is the notion of aesthetic, that brings the concept and principles of beauty and human purpose within reach, that are characteristic of the social and physical worlds inhabited by humans. Literature and the arts are activities that propel history forward by the design and production of objects that concentrate experience, expose key ideas and contradictions, raise ethical concerns and awaken curiosity and enthusiasm for social change and improvement. Embedded in literature and arts are the stories and lessons that have accumulated over centuries assisting current practice and the resolution of problems that are encountered every day.

In many respects, incorporation of the arts from various cultural perspectives into the regular school curriculum, indeed as the basis of the regular school curriculum, should be a relatively straight forward proposition. Different forms of expression have evolved from within different cultures, languages and perceptions situated within different political, economic and natural landscapes, but such perceptions can be similar. Perceptions involving connection, grief, aggression, excitement, uncertainty and the like. Most education systems of the world include studies of literature and the arts for all children recognising their importance in developing a heightened awareness of society past and present and the values of human conduct that are considered appropriate. Similar to their non-Indigenous cousins, Indigenous communities pursue literary and artistic activity through various forms of story-telling, writing, painting, singing and dancing and ceremony and with a particular role for Elders in providing continuity and wisdom. In terms of dance for example, the Indigenous Australian choreographer, Stephen Page (Bangarra, 2020) and the African American, Alvin Ailey (2020), both aim to express and communicate non-dominant culture to national and international audiences through dance and movement. Page works to communicate with remote Indigenous communities, urban Indigenous communities and wider Australia. He also honours the collaboration of Indigenous cultures of Australia and as well as challenging non-Indigenous Australians he also challenges Indigenous Australians to rethink their identity. In similar manner, Ailey said that one of America's richest treasures was the African-American cultural heritage— 'sometimes sorrowful, sometimes jubilant, but always hopeful.' His work is a tribute to that tradition, born out of the choreographer's 'blood memories' of his childhood in rural Texas and the Baptist Church. Ailey's signature ballet, 'Revelations,' since its premiere in 1960, has been performed continuously around the globe, transcending barriers of faith and nationality, and appealing to universal emotions, making it the most widely-seen modern dance work in the world.

The fact that the general human practice of literature and arts has evolved as a general philosophy of practice for all communities around the world is testament to its significance for human existence and the ongoing quest for meaning and purpose. There is a deep human need and imperative to move beyond the immediate and apparently mundane, to a wholeness and universal that uplifts and pervades human consciousness.

1   Picasso and Namatjira

At some time in the future, it may be possible that distinctions between various forms of knowledge as we know them at present, will disappear. That is, it will be recognised and accepted that all humans go about interacting with the world in an intellectual or cognitive sense, in the same manner. This has enormous implications for schools, because it means that how students engage what we now call mathematics, language, science, humanities, arts and the like will be the same, regardless of the specific topics of the curriculum. Integrated knowledge and inquiry learning will have been achieved. Until that time is reached, the profession needs to agree on accurate definitions of each subject area so that practitioners have available to them a coherent and consistent framework within which to act. Biesta (2018, p. 14) for example, suggests that definitions pertaining to the arts that emphasise creativity and expression do not necessarily raise questions about the *quality* of these features and instead, that focus needs to highlight the '*existential quality* of what and who is being expressed, a quality that has to do with how children and young people can *exist* well, individually and collectively, *in* the word and *with* the world.' Further discussion will be undertaken on these issues below, but for the moment it should be noted that Biesta has taken an educational stance on the question of the role of the arts in schools and has identified existence as their central purpose. He asks how can the arts assist children and young people to live well, both in and with the world? From a philosophical perspective, this could be detailed to reflect on the meaning of human existence, of experiencing mind, to act, think and create, ethically. This is not an abstract or idealist contention, but arises from our material interaction with the world, its histories, cultures and problems, every day.

Generally considered as an icon of the 20th century, Pablo Picasso (1881–1973) and his art ushered in a new way of seeing what is real (Picasso, 2018). His 1907 painting entitled *Les Demoiselles d'Avignon* (The Young Ladies of Avignon) shows five nude female prostitutes from Barcelona with angular body shapes and faces that appear provocative and mask-like. This was Picasso's break with the then current and major European style of Naturalism and extended the interpretation of Impressionism. It introduced what one critic termed Cubism, due to the preponderance of geometric lines and shapes and attempted to depict and reassemble the main characteristics of the subject. Picasso is said to have commented that 'I paint objects as I think them, not as I see them.' Many years later, Picasso was to utilise this style in perhaps his most famous painting that portrayed Nazi bombing of the Spanish village of Guernica in 1937. In this large black and white representation, Picasso uses dramatic images of the bull and horse to depict fighting to the death, a dismembered soldier and figures of women who are attempting to cope with violence and destruction. Within such slaughter, a small flower struggles to survive, a sign of hope amongst the debris. By his painting of *Guernica,* Picasso demonstrated the role of art in bringing into stark relief the depths to which humanity can fall, but at the same time, can stir within us deep feelings of compassion and what the human spirit can endure. Picasso lived during times of war and great upheaval and his art reflected corresponding changes in his own thinking. There is always tension between what we observe and how that is expressed, how different perspectives are brought to bear on events, how the boundaries of understanding can be extended into what is new and challenging. We suspect that Picasso was coming to terms with events in his own life when he broke away from convention and pushed forward with the new style of Cubism. This did not occur quickly, without personal doubt and public criticism, but it eventually enabled Picasso and many artists who followed, to respect their own artistic endeavours, thinking and imaginative insight to understand the social and physical worlds with greater independence and clarity. That is, to understand themselves.

For the non-Indigenous observer, Indigenous art can be appreciated, but not understood. This may be the case with all art of course, where what the artist has in mind may be quite different to what the bystander sees and comprehends. The use of materials such as cloth, straw, paint, stone, wood and clay enable different interpretations of ideas and events to be formatted so that main features can be represented and communicated. A photograph of a person may capture the characteristics of a person, a moment in time, whereas a portrait may bring to light what the painter perceives as human qualities existing deep inside. Picasso's 1905 painting of the American writer and benefactor Gertrude Stein being a case in point. Like *Guernica*, Indigenous painting can be telling a story of history, community, of grief and hardship, or delight and solidarity. In this sense, it crosses the boundaries between literature and art. The Australian Indigenous painter, Albert Namatjira (1902–1959), who was born in the desert country of Central Australia, was a contemporary artist of the outback landscape. Using soft water colours, Namatjira depicted the purple hills, orange sandstone, grey-green foliage and clear water holes of his homeland, often framed by large, distinctive white ghost gum trees of the interior. Namatjira was introduced to this essentially European style of painting by the non-Indigenous Australian landscape painter, Rex Battarbee (Edmund, 2014) who, like many Australian artists, went to central Australia to experience unique country, the brilliance of natural light and the surrounding remoteness. Whether intended or otherwise and to the non-Indigenous eye, Namatjira's paintings draw the observer into landscape, connect with country and project a feeling of familiarity not known before. Colours, form and impressions provide some understanding of the Indigenous concept of being, of being 'of the land.' Albert Namatjira may have been committing his truth to canvas, of bringing what he felt and understood alive for others to contemplate and wonder. That is, of depicting personal truth as reality as we exist in a universal wholeness, accepted as real, subjectively and objectively, but beyond our formal comprehension.

2   School Education and the Arts

In a small, fascinating book, Biesta (2017) reminds us of a famous performance presentation in 1965 by the German artist Joseph Beuys entitled *How to explain pictures to a dead hare*. In this performance piece, Beuys could be viewed by spectators through the galley's windows, his head and face covered in honey and gold leaf, a slab of iron tied to one boot, a felt pad to the other, as the artist cradled a dead hare. Beuys frequently whispered things to the animal carcass about his own drawings hanging on the walls around him. He would periodically vary the bleak rhythm of this scenario by walking around the cramped space, one footstep muffled by felt, the other amplified by iron. Honey was chosen to represent life, gold for wealth, hare as death, metal as conductor of invisible energies and felt as protection. Beuys wanted to demonstrate the visceral connections produced by art rather than the rational, intellectual and therefore, by definition, his performance needed to raise confusion and interpretation (as it does to this day). In pondering what Beuys might have intended, Biesta (2017, pp. 44–48) suggests that the performance is first and foremost an 'archetypical form of showing,' whereby one person shows something of worth to another, where a person is drawn 'into reason' or sense-making as explanation for themselves, where pictures are used to accompany explanation. Biesta comments that the dead hare indicates that the artist or teacher cannot control where learning and understanding are concerned, what is grasped depends on the participant, as subject. Art is a form of teaching and learning that must constitute freedom.

Indigenous art does not have to conform to non-Indigenous understandings, but where the regular school curriculum is concerned, with Indigenous students in the minority more often than not, there needs to be overlap and connection. Each can learn from and appreciate the other. That is, when art does not merely present preformed objects, but contributes to the formation of freedom. The esteemed Welsh sociologist, Raymond Williams spoke of culture in the following manner, with the general characteristics easily being applied to art. Williams (1961, as cited by Pring, 2013, p. 46) noted that culture involves:

> the body of intellectual and imaginative work, in which, in a detailed way, human thought and experience are variously recorded ... the activity of criticism, by which the nature of thought and experience, the details of the language, form and convention in which these are active are described and valued.

Like mathematics (see Chapter 5), schools do not have to pay a great deal of attention to the philosophy of knowledge if they so choose and instead, can concentrate on the transmission of packaged content. Schools do not have to recognise for each student as Pring notes that they are working with 'a body of intellectual and imaginative work' that has accrued over a lifetime, involving 'thought, experience, language, form and convention' that is peculiar for each person. To take these issues and those raised in the chapters of this book as guidance, a definition of arts is now advanced for consideration by schools:

> That the arts involve deliberate human activity enabling subjective awareness for artist and observer to occur when the objects of activity are experienced.

For schools, this definition draws a distinction between the arts and sciences, where the latter can be restricted to the investigation of causes and facts regarding the natural world. The notion of being 'deliberate' means activity involving specified subject content that is more open-ended and personal with creative and innovative intent. Finally, it is recognised that there is an intimate relationship between participants and the objects of activity that encourage enhanced human subjectivity of being with the world, of being an organic subject and not an isolated object. Listening to music, moving to the rhythms of dance, reading a story, weaving a basket, designing a fabric, interpretating a role for dramatic performance, wondering at the contours and patterns of the earth, all evoke personal connections with the characteristics of the material objects being encountered, a deeper relationship with the unity of the cosmos. Bearing in mind the comment from Raymond Williams (1958) that 'culture is the whole of life,' it is difficult to restrict any definition of the arts to particular activity, but in this case, specific consideration is being given to curriculum and how schools can conceptualise the purpose of arts and assessment of outcomes.

The proposed definition above links language, literature and the arts. Literature is a generic term, taken to mean the stories spoken, written and variously expressed by children and communities, rather than a superior form of artistic endeavour, assumed as 'high culture and arts.' Language, literature and the arts are therefore combined in many ways, in drawing and painting, in story telling around the camp fire or kitchen table where community and family histories are described and explained and where participants are invited into the great journeys of humankind. This process exists in the sciences as well where qualitative and quantitative results are discussed and disputed for interpretation and meaning. It goes to the heart of Kuhn's 'paradigm shift,' where current approaches in science are seen to be incommensurate with new evidence, precipitating new thinking. For example, Paul Jennings, the Australian writer of short stories for children relates what happened when he began writing scripts for a childrens' television series. He suggests that if you don't have a good story well told, then 'you have nothing' (Jennings, 2020, p. 242):

> At the first reading of my first script, I spoke nervously. I said that I didn't want pitfalls and slapstick comedy. The humour was sophisticated and

contained in the writing. Just because the viewers were children didn't mean that the acting had to be childish. The jokes had to be good enough to make adults laugh too. I also pointed out that this particular genre, contemporary fantasy, depended on the background world appearing to be normal and believable. I wanted the school to be a typical school. And the teachers to be real teachers, not fools. The environment could be ten percent removed from reality, but no more.

In this extract, Jennings is entirely respectful of children and their intellect, arguing that writing for them needs to be 'sophisticated' with the context 'normal and believable.' Jennings is noted for his stories containing unusual plots to involve children and to highlight and maintain their interests, rather than being simplistic and 'childish.' This requires a deep understanding of children and their activity. These characteristics could be seen as being central to the *Harry Potter* series as well, although having a greater emphasis on fantasy, magic, myth and folklore. In the broad sense, language, literature and storytelling infuse all the arts, in all cultures around the world: they embody what it means to be human and what it means to experience and express our humanity. Accordingly, it is not a big step to envisage language, literature and the arts as forms of acting, thinking and expressing infusing all subject content across the curriculum and thereby eliciting more profound understandings of what are considered to be major ideas and practices. This leads to a much more holistic view of knowledge, firmly located in culture and initially, thoroughly informal, ordinary, personal and constructed. Perhaps the opposite of the regular curriculum imposed on children around the world. In a powerful statement, Dewey (1934/2005, p. 254) would agree with this perspective, as he provides summary comment about human communication and its central positioning in the arts:

> People associate in many ways. But the only form of association that is truly human and not a gregarious gathering for warmth and protection, or a mere device for efficiency in outer action, is the participation in meanings and goods that is effected by communication. The expressions that constitute art are communication in its pure and undefiled form.

In this way, Dewey is drawing attention to the moral and humane qualities inherent in the arts and, as such, are important practices and possibilities arising from what he calls 'an experience.' He points out the place of communication within all the arts whereby humans connect and express intellectual and social meaning. We all participate with the activities of daily life at school, home and community, much of which may seemingly pass us by, in the moment. However the significance of 'an experience' occurs when we are sensitive to and are touched by our communicative engagement with the world, the notion of 'subjective awareness' taken from our definition above. It seems clear that the arts must take their equal place with other areas of curriculum and pedagogy and not be relegated to a subservient position by impoverished neoliberal ideology.

3 Praxis Philosophy of Arts

Learning from the land is a central principle of life for Indigenous peoples and, I suspect, for all peoples. For schools, this principle needs to be incorporated across the curriculum for all staff and children to become closer to the holistic world, to enhance personal subjectivities. In writing about subjectivity and the human aesthetic, or what it means to be aware of and concerned with beauty and its appreciation, to be sensitive to taste, or the qualities of a particular artistic endeavour, Dewey (1934/2005, p. 143) outlined what he considered to be necessary conditions to bring 'an experience' to its conclusion:

> Such characteristics as continuity, cumulation, conservation, tension and anticipation are thus formal conditions of aesthetic form. The factor of resistance is worth special notice at this point. Without internal tension there would be a fluid rush to a straightaway mark; there would be nothing that could be called development and fulfillment. The existence of resistance defines the place of intelligence in the production of an object of fine art.

In his discussion of Dewey's approach to aesthetic form, Jackson (1998, pp. 45–54) notes that continuity refers to 'what is stable in experience,' the physical factors, habits and ideas that endure through change and time. The buildup that occurs as a work of art is advanced for both artist and observer, results in cumulation, or an increase in the sense of worth, 'a progressive massing of values.' Exhibition of Picasso's *Guernica,* or of Namatjira's water colours would certainly culminate in excitement and discussion of meaning as communities gathered to view the final product. In regards conservation, Dewey saw contradictory energies operating within art experience without which the experience would collapse or dissipate, artistic fulfillment denied. Dewey may have been drawing upon the idea of dialectic here, with all experience requiring movement and transformation. His notion of energies may have referred to the features of materials being used and the different ideas that arise when forming and working with such materials: what is possible with marble, is different to what is possible with wood. The opposition of energies can also be referred to as tension, where there is compression of tension seeking release. According to Jackson, Dewey explains that 'During compression, the condition of intensity dominates. During release, the shift is to extensity.' This movement can be felt in a piece of music, where there can be escalation of rhythm and tempo, followed by a change of key or modulation to produce a contrary effect, the rise and fall of heartbeat. Anticipation occurs throughout this time, before the experience has formally begun and then during the experience itself. Dewey contends that both artist and audience are uncertain of the aesthetic experience as it unfolds, but both can anticipate what might be coming next. Biesta (2018, pp. 15–16) takes up the issue of resistance in art as 'encounter with the world,' such that when we meet opposition, criticism, or countervailing views, 'we experience that the world is not a construction and particularly, not our construction, but that it exists in its own right.' When this occurs, decisions and judgements must be made about how to proceed with what is 'real,' how to make our own way in relation to others. At these times, the conditions and movements of the human aesthetic come into play.

Taking the above discussion into account regarding art and aesthetics for all children in schools, for children of Indigenous and non-Indigenous origins, it is possible to conceptualise a philosophy of practice for language, literature and art, a holistic and inclusive philosophy of praxis (see Chapter 6, for discussion of pragmatism and praxis). Hooley (2018, pp. 156–157) notes praxis for schools as 'cycles of ethically framed action or rationality regarding what is good and appropriate, based on a system of values and judgement rather than rules or laws to improve teaching and learning,' such that, 'a major philosophical leap is being made.' He goes on to describe schooling as therefore being 'imbued with a moral purpose about what teaching and learning are for in the mutual interests of participants.' By incorporating Indigenous ways of knowing within the definition of arts suggested above (That the arts involve deliberate human activity enabling subjective awareness for artist and observer to occur when the objects of activity are experienced), the practices, values and judgements of Indigenous and non-Indigenous students can be respected and underpin all learning. In understanding language, literature and art as holistic praxis experience involving continuity, cumulation, conservation, anticipation and resistance, school learning undertakes a dramatic shift. While previously being overly concerned with the transmission of dominate culture and economics, it transforms to being concerned with experience of living in and with the world, for personal realisation of what it means to be fully subjective, community and human. To be alive, is to live in this way.

4 Excursus 3: Tower Hill

It's always good to be heading home, away from the big city and towards the freshness of rolling surf and golden sands. Those words from Banjo Paterson's famous poem usually ringing in my ears: '… and the foetid air and gritty/of the dusty dirty city/through the open window floating/spreads its foulness over all.' While my favourite place was the beach of my childhood, the country town was surrounded by green and lush dairy pasture with stands of European and Australian gum trees scattered across the landscape. I decided to take a slight detour before visiting my parents and instead, made my way to the lip of an extinct volcano a few kilometres from town. Tower Hill is thought to have last erupted about 32,000 years ago and, in the early years of European settlement in the area, much of the vegetation then present was cleared for farming. From 1961, a major replanting program was undertaken, guided by a painting by the Austrian artist Eugene von Guerard in 1855. I had often viewed this painting hanging in the local art gallery, imagining von Guerard walking through rugged countryside and recording its formation in fine detail, that of hills, rivers, waterfalls and bush. The coastal wind whipped at my coat as I walked over to the edge of the crater and the full expanse of the volcano spread out before me. It was obvious that the wattles, banksias, eucalypts and other plants had grown considerably since my last visit and were covering the cones and valleys of the volcano. I could just see the visitors' centre where local Indigenous people often provided guided tours and introduced the emu, kangaroo and koala residents. What were Indigenous stories about the origin of this distinctive landscape I wondered. Surveying this scene always gave me a strange feeling, of looking back in time and wondering what von Guerard was thinking as he stood on this very spot and sketched, painted and interpreted what he saw. He probably contrasted the light and flora with his European background, and like me, thinking new thoughts about land and existence. It was an emotional time, I felt at home, where I needed to be, close to what I knew in a personal sense, much more than my somewhat artificial place in the city. I had asked myself these questions many times before, but as I turned to leave, the answers remained elusive. My consciousness in motion shaped by the sights and sounds of Tower Hill.

CHAPTER 4

Redefining School Mathematics as Philosophy of Practice

> Nevertheless, those with the greatest stake in sovereignty for Indigenous peoples – that is Indigenous peoples themselves – need more than a spirt of resistance, they need a pedagogical structure that provides methods of inquiry and analysis that exposes, challenges and disrupts the continuing colonisation of their lands and resources.
>
> SANDY GRANDE

∴

Mathematics is one of the great intellectual achievements of humankind, but its essential character remains somewhat shadowy and mysterious. On the one hand, it is practical and everyday, allowing us to think about the time it takes to walk to school, or how spiders build their webs? On the other, what is the meaning of number, or do circles actually exist? Humans have thought about these ideas for centuries, including the Greek philosopher Plato, who considered ideal objects or forms that related to our direct experience of them. We have an understanding of number or hexagon in our minds (the idea, or form), but what we encounter in reality is an approximation of the ideal. Some scholars consider mathematics to be absolute truth, or human attempts at understanding the universe completely and accurately. Rather than being absolute, other philosophers see mathematics as being fallible and corrigible, always capable of revision and correction, tentative acceptance or rejection. Accordingly, there is more than one concept of mathematics such as empiricism, formalism, logicism, intuitionism and constructivism making the choice of approach adopted by schools a difficult decision indeed. Interestingly, most schooling systems around the world, supported by the education profession, have decided on the same, conservative and behaviouristic perspective of school mathematical content, teaching and learning.

There is no reason to expect that mathematical knowledge is not of the same configuration as all other expressions of human knowledge. The intellectual capability for all humans to think mathematically and to engage mathematical knowledge, is therefore the same, there is no concept of deficit. That is, if we view knowledge as the process by which our internal reality (perceptions, conceptions) connects with external reality (physical, social worlds). In this sense, the production of mathematical knowledge is a social process, rather than one where knowledge is held by some authority and transmitted to others; we each construct our own understandings. Not all philosophers of course have neglected the social aspects of knowledge, or of mathematical knowledge. Specifically, the content of mathematics is seen to include shapes, patterns, quantities and their relationships. Dewey for example was very clear about the central role social experience plays in knowledge production. Freire argued the place of community, culture, language and dialogue in knowing and learning. What this means is that we conceptualise mathematical knowledge as arising from social constructivism, or collaborative action by every citizen, the same as all other knowledges. Why should mathematical knowledge be considered as being different? A good example of this understanding (discussed below) is called *ethnomathematics* which, as the name suggests, means mathematical knowledge arising from the ethnic background, cultures and languages of particular groups of people. Ethnomathematics is well known in South America and draws upon the community, craft and agricultural experiences of the people, for example, the patterns of weaved clothing, baskets and mats, the structure of terraced fields, musical instruments, farming implements, stone walls and bridges, weapons of aggression and the like. Mathematics as a process of investigating shapes, patterns and quantities is not so much a process of constant calculation disconnected from social life, but of thinking about how the universe works and therefore, how to guide personal and community interest.

1 Indigenous Approaches to School Mathematics

In terms of mathematics curriculum in schools, the immersion in a numerate and literate culture as represented in formal school knowledge, may not be part of the habitus of many communities that do not live as part of, or necessarily accept the dominant mores of mainstream society. For example, the Indigenous Australian academic Matthews (2019) makes the case for mathematics generally to be considered a cultural activity:

> To see and understand an Indigenous perspective of mathematics, you must accept the premise that mathematics is intrinsically connected to culture and, consequently, has many different cultural expressions.

A common perception is that mathematics, as well as science, is objective, culture and value free. Objectivity is often seen as the foundation of mathematics and science because it is believed that it leads to absolute facts and truths. However I would contend that all knowledge systems are bound by culture, including mathematics and once its subjectivity is embraced, there is a much richer, diverse knowledge system to engage with and understand.

In this statement, Matthews is adding to the position mentioned above that what we call mathematical knowledge is engaged by all in the same way as other knowledges, by claiming it is shaped and formed by culture. This is the essential understanding when Indigenous children are attending non-Indigenous schools and connections are being investigated between the regular curriculum and the experiences of Indigenous students. It may be for example that the concept of gravity as a scientific entity can be directly related to daily life for most children, such as the observation that the leaves of the tree, or the pen pushed off the table, fall down, towards the earth, rather than up, towards the sky. The reason for this can be theorised through the idea of 'force' acting in a certain way, perhaps a difficult idea for all children of a certain age and background. Mathematics is a different case, when ideas and their relationships are expressed in symbols and can then be manipulated under various conditions, $F = ma$ for instance. To have some understanding of this relationship demands some equivalent understanding of force, mass and acceleration and what might happen when their values are altered. A set of symbols such as $y = 3x + 7$ has further complications when unknowns depicted with x and y are included. Algebraic equations may be important to the engineer, but less so for the Year 9 child. There is an argument that regardless of cultural background, we can all appreciate the different concepts that exist around the world of the same phenomenon. It may not be possible for any person or group to have exactly the same concept of gravity or force, but be able to be sensitive towards the meanings of others. What becomes problematic and indeed discriminatory, is when particular viewpoints and meanings are imposed by social systems and must be accepted in their precise disposition.

Culture, then, is central to and tempers all learning, in all countries and including children of the dominant society. As noted by Matthews, in most countries, mathematics is often thought to be objective, the basis of facts and truth, perhaps the opposite of culture that involves opinion, emotion and direct experience. However this distinction between the objective and subjective can be seen as false. It may be agreed that Paris is the capital city of France, that water boils at 100 degrees Celsius, that Mount Everest is the highest mountain in the world, that Nelson Mandela was the President of South Africa, but there is the question of how these 'facts' became known and what preceded them? These statements are 'facts' in the sense that they guide human action and understanding, but 'facts' can change over time. That is, they are not 'facts' without context, or without meaning, they are not 'facts' that must be accepted uncritically or not be interpreted for their continuing use in social practice. Rather, each person brings to bear what they think about such 'facts and truths' as they function in the world with them. Objective researchers who measure objects do so in the same way, they measure from their previous knowledge and experience, making interpretations and judgements as they proceed. From a dialectical point of view, personal human understanding occurs from a constant interaction of the objective and subjective, bringing forth the new thoughts and ideas that inform human consciousness. This social act of knowledge production involves human action of engaging, reflecting and interpreting the social and physical worlds. It is a dialectical social process of collaborative experience, where all of us from different cultures, languages and histories relate and interrelate with the world in a human way, as we construct and reconstruct what it means to be human. How can mathematics be excluded from this process?

It is extremely difficult of course for any education system operating within a dominant economic and political context, to respect and incorporate different cultural perspectives, especially when their world views are contradictory. Formation of rivers by geological movement of the land, is a different philosophy to the river being channelled by the foraging of large fish. There are two ways of proceeding to be culturally respectful. First, to attempt to 'Indigenise' the curriculum, whereby one cultural view of knowledge essentially replaces another. It could be argued that this approach will not occur unless the current economic and political structure is overthrown and will permit a different culture to exist. Second, to provide a set of similar ideas and principles that can link the knowledges and practices of each culture, known generally as 'two-way learning.' Here, the dominant culture retains its position, especially if formal examinations are involved. In relation to the 'two-way' approach, Beatty (2016) comments:

> Indigenous pedagogy emphasises experiential learning, modelling and collaborative activity. Community members used a combination of direct instruction to teach activity-based skills and informal inquiry into mathematical problems that naturally arose from the activities, for example, calculating the ratio of beads to centimetre to determine the length students needed to make their loomed bracelets. Students worked

with community members in small groups or individually to find solutions and the Native members of the research team described how this was similar to learning experiences they had experienced as children working with Elders.

Even the small changes described by Beatty for Native Canadians children may be unrealistic for many schools. Change must start with a great idea. However what she reports is small groups of students working with community members on mutual interest, drawing on the broad understanding of citizens. This occurs within the framework of what others have experienced and recommended through the ages. Mathematical knowledge and practice is perhaps the most difficult area of the school curriculum for inclusion in an Indigenous framework of teaching and learning. There seems to be an assumption that Plato lives on, that mathematics is a timeless truth that holds for everyone, all over the world. Some teachers who may adopt an inquiry-type approach to knowledge in some of their subjects, can revert to a logical positivist view when they walk into the mathematics classroom. In many areas of the school curriculum, a few intellectual building blocks are used to create and express the cascading of human curiosity and imagination, whereas in school mathematics, the never-ending algorithms are imposed and seldom used to build anything creative and innovative. At least, to build something that is personal, dynamic and generative. If mathematics can be considered as cultural, uncertain and ambiguous – a reasonable guide to human interaction with the universe, but uncertain and ambiguous nevertheless – then all subject content in the school curriculum can be considered as being uncertain as well. As soon as this position is adopted to one extent or another, there are serious revolutionary implications for how knowledge is structured, organised and assessed in all subjects, in all schools.

In noting that Improving educational outcomes for Pasifika (various ethnic groups who are first generation Pacific or New Zealand-born with Pacific ancestry or heritage) learners is a national priority in New Zealand, Taeao and Averill (2019) suggest that looking beyond usual pedagogies may be essential for enhancing Pasifika student learning. For culturally responsive purposes, they investigated using dance as a pedagogy for mathematics learning for Pasifika and other students. A common form of (Pacific Islander) Samoan dance called sāsā was studied as it tells a story through actions that depict Samoan histories, practices and daily activities. The sāsā is performed in unison, with clarity and commitment, and represents the Samoan value of collectivism. Number sense through rhythm and combined rhythm of the dance using clapping games and exploring symmetries, shapes and geometric concepts through choreography involving hand, arm and body movements. Connecting principles of school mathematics with dance movement, music and rhythm integrates what people know (or are in the process of knowing) with what they are doing, making the abstract concrete (Taeao & Averill, 2019):

> Dance provides opportunities to draw from the cultural capital and funds of knowledge of Pasifika learners, their families and members of the community. Pasifika dance has the potential to be useful for teaching mathematical concepts such as geometry, symmetry, shapes, angles, fractions and number patterns through choreography and movement. Using dance as a pedagogy has the potential to nurture students' emotional, physical, social and spiritual wellbeing and to connect Pasifika traditions and knowledge with mathematics learning.

If the concept of 'learning from the land' is considered, then an environment described for Pasifika students can be easily be apprehended, demanding creative responses on a daily basis. Reading the land, knowing its stories and histories, linking weather changes and animal behaviour, knowing where to find food and water, constructing events through observation of signs and tracks, all contribute to mathematical acts of understanding, mathematical thinking. When following this type of approach, the school is contributing to an environment of inquiry that encourages students to investigate what they know and don't know about their lives from the point of view of their personal cultures and knowledges. Mathematical thinking and practice becomes a part of 'how we are.'

2   Ethnomathematics, a Cultural View of Mathematics

Originating in South America in the 1980s, ethnomathematics provides a particular way of thinking about mathematics that may challenge traditional approaches in schools and universities so that the field becomes more inclusive of diverse views and practices. In discussing what he broadly termed 'academic mathematics' which is taught and learned in most schools around the world, D'Ambrosio (1997, p. 16) commented:

> In contrast to this, we will call ethnomathematics the mathematics which is practised among identifiable cultural groups, such as national tribal societies, labour groups, children of a certain age bracket, professional classes and so on. Its identity depends largely on focuses of interest, on

motivation and on certain codes and jargons which do not belong to the realm of academic mathematics. We may go even further in this concept of ethnomathematics to include much of the mathematics which is currently practised by engineers, mainly calculus, which does not respond to the concept of rigour and formalism developed in academic courses of calculus.

As a major and founding theorist regarding ethnomathematics, this is an astounding statement by D'Ambrosio. It has a very broad understanding of culture, arguing that different groups of people based on tribal association, social class, ethnicity, age and occupation will approach mathematical practice differently. This supports the notion mentioned previously that mathematical knowledge is the same as other knowledges where understanding is constructed by each person based on their current experience, that is a cultural view of knowledge. It is the prerogative of each society to decide how knowledge is to be arranged across its schooling systems and how children are to be introduced to ideas of increasing complexity and ideas that are not generally encountered within a specific cultural context. This point is raised by D'Ambrosio above where he alludes to more informal approaches adopted by engineers as distinct from the 'concept of rigour and formalism' that is characteristic of 'academic' programs of study. In some respects, this concept can be related to the issue of 'facts' noted earlier, where accepted ways of acting are followed, but there is room for flexible, imaginative and inspirational thinking to fit particular circumstances and when problems occur. A large building that is sinking into the ground requires innovative decision-making to support the substructures, in the same way that creative diagnosis is required for a sick child, or a motor that will not start. Being able to think and work in this way, 'to think on your feet,' to reflect in and on action, does require a thorough understanding of the issues involved, but when considering the schooling of children, their participation with their own culture and knowledge should come first, with more formal and abstract ideas coming later. That is, personal meaning of situations needs to be constructed in relation to the issues being investigated, rather than having predetermined ideas imposed.

Regardless of respect for Indigenous or traditional people and knowledge systems, there is an equally large question at stake here involving the mathematical thinking that resides in the heads of all people both within and between cultures and how these can or should be reconciled for mutual understanding. In a fascinating study that looked at how an Indigenous group of people in the Philippines used mathematical ideas when building stone walls, Alangui (2003, p. 61) reported that: 'The idea of friction seems to be captured in the way they describe the positioning of stones, that is when they talk about the stones as "biting into each other," or "tightening like screws."' This example certainly shows non-European people utilising ideas that are also clearly European-mathematical and, no doubt, ideas that have been in the common vernacular for hundreds of years. In a similar manner, Francois and Stathopoulou report on their research with Romany children in Greece and their approach to mathematics. Romany (or Traveller, Gypsy) families have a semi-nomadic way of life that may result in irregular school attendance and are strongly family-oriented including community and work activities. While it is often mentioned in the mathematics curriculum of schools around the world that connections should be made between everyday knowledge and academic knowledge, Francois and Stathopoulou (2012, p. 243) state that, for their participants:

> Based on the results of our research observations we have to conclude that this way of leaning did not occur. Students had no chance to exploit their out of school experience and to develop a dialectic relationship between their community identity and their identity as mathematics learners. Even though culturally acquired, informal cognition can inform the formal one in particular situations which helas normally doesn't happen since teachers are strictly limited to formal procedures. Formal education, as expressed through the teacher, either ignore or contemn this background cognition of Romany students.

In taking up the concept of ethnomathematics to combat the range of issues noted in this extract, it may be appropriate to give greater definition to what might be called Indigenomathematics for Indigenous students specifically. As discussed by Hooley (2010, pp. 228–231), land, culture and language are placed at the centre of Indigenous life and consequently must be placed at the centre of the mathematics curriculum. He points out that given the different circumstances of urban, regional and remote communities, the task of providing qualified teachers and appropriate materials in support of Indigenous philosophy will not be easy to meet. There will need to be respectful and continuing discussions between schools and local communities to identify key issues of interest and concern and how these can link to the regular curriculum. In the first instance, there will need to be consensus around the formation of a philosophical framework of knowledge to guide curriculum development. One experiential pedagogical feature that will need to be incorporated is that of story telling, or narrative, undertaken by small groups of learning circles. As mentioned above, there are difficult and contested issues of objectivity and subjectivity at stake here, with Indigenous people arguing no doubt, that Indigenous knowledge does not require non-Indigenous approval, but can stand alongside other ideas and principles accepted by the regular curriculum. As the main feature of Indigenomathematics, theorising knowledge connections with the land, culture and language will fundamentally change the nature of school mathematics, creating a genuine field of philosophical practice for Indigenous and non-Indigenous children alike.

3 Wittgenstein and the Foundations of Mathematics

Often referred to as one of the most important and controversial philosophers of the 20th Century, Ludwig Wittgenstein (1889–1951) set about redefining philosophy as philosophy of language. His two books published thirty years apart in 1921 and 1953 took opposing positions on the question of language and demonstrated his change in thinking throughout his lifetime on the nature of philosophy. As a young engineer, Wittgenstein had initially visited the British philosopher Bertrand Russell at Cambridge in 1911 to discuss with him the philosophy of mathematics and expressly, mathematical logic. Russell had recently published *Principia Mathematica* that remains a central text in the philosophy of mathematics today. Over the years, Wittgenstein moved away from Russell's analytical approach and adopted a much more open and interpretive meaning of mathematics, based on the use of language by each individual person. In this regard, Wittgenstein did not distinguish between different knowledges and did not isolate mathematics as a special case.

A major difference between Wittgenstein and Russell was whether mathematics had what is called foundational knowledge, that is whether there existed in the universe, a set of baseline 'truths' from which mathematics as a knowledge discipline could be constructed. If so, then mathematics itself could be considered as 'truth' for humans to follow. For example, Newton's laws of gravitation could be seen as guiding the motion of planets through the skies, or alternatively, could be taken as guiding human understanding of the motion of cosmic bodies. If the latter, then Newton's laws provide a way of thinking about what we observe, rather than constitute laws that determine how the universe functions. Whether it is agreed that there is foundational knowledge or mathematical truth, or not, has tremendous significance for school mathematics, given that most programs of school mathematics around the world seem to accept the former proposition. As noted above, Plato's concept of 'ideal forms' comes into play where, although access to the ideal forms is not possible, approximations can be envisaged for humans. When looking at the moon at night, children can be told that they are looking at a circle, but whether ideal circles actually exist for human experience, is doubtful. Wittgenstein's work with language indicated that foundational knowledge for mathematics does not occur, lending support to the view that mathematics like all knowledge arises from cultural experience and tentative social 'truths' that endure until such time as the evidence changes. The earth is considered flat until such time as it is considered not.

Wittgenstein's thinking and writing is not easy to follow and understand. It is therefore open to continuing contest and interpretation. He writes in short, numbered sentences that often seem disconnected to everything else and are written as they occur to him; there is little if any explanation of meaning. Frustratingly, there is little indication of where his thought is heading. This style is most evident in his first book known as the *Tractatus* (Wittgenstein, 1921), where he outlines his concept of language involving words being used to name objects and pictures of objects are generated. In the *Tractatus*, we find the following:

> 2.1 We make to ourselves pictures of facts.
> 2.11 The picture presents the facts in logical space, the existence and non-existence of atomic facts.
> 2.12 The picture is a model of reality.
> 2.13 To the objects correspond in the picture the elements of the picture.
> 2.131 The elements of the picture stand, in the picture, for the objects.
> 2.14 The picture consists in the fact that its elements are combined with one another in a definite way.
> 2.141 The picture is a fact.

Perhaps demonstrating the influence of Russell at this stage, this approach to language is assuredly analytical, stepwise, with readers being left to their own devices regarding what the author was intending. However his view altered dramatically. Before his second book was published, Wittgenstein had a range of personal experiences that may explain his change in thinking, where he moved between an academic position at Cambridge, being a school teacher in a small Austrian rural village, designing a house in fine detail for his sister (reflecting his early work and interest in engineering and aeronautics) and seriously doubting his progress in redefining philosophy, seriously doubting himself. In his later life, he came to the view that philosophy was about the clarification of language, such that when a problem could be expressed without ambiguity, the problem was understood and solved. It may be that Wittgenstein was exhibiting this style in his written work, where he was attempting to display ideas as clearly as possible and it was up to the reader to clarify their own ideas and conceptions accordingly. In the most famous and final statement from the *Tractatus,* Wittgenstein submits an amazing challenge:

> 6.54 My propositions are elucidatory in this way: he who understands me finally recognises them as senseless, when he has climbed out through them, on them, over them. (He must so to speak throw away the ladder, after he has climbed up on it.) 7 Whereof one cannot speak, thereof one must be silent.

Readers are enjoined here to understand Wittgenstein as being 'senseless' for them and then to proceed to work out for themselves what they think and understand. His view is entirely analytic when he states that if we do not understand an issue, then we must be silent about it, rather than it seems, engaging in discussion with others to investigate what the issue is about, to compare and contrast different views and to develop tentative ideas until such time as experience determines otherwise. If this interpretation is reasonably accurate, then by the time his second book, *Philosophical Investigations* (Wittgenstein, 1953) was published, Wittgenstein had a different view of what humans were all about. He introduces his notion of 'language games':

> 7. In the practice of the use of language, one party calls out the words, the other acts on them. In instruction in the language, the following process will occur: the learner names the objects; that is, he utters the word when the teacher points to the stone. And there will be this still simpler exercise: the pupil repeats the words after the teacher – both of these being processes resembling language. We can also think of the whole process of using words as one of those games by means of which children learn their native language. I will call these games 'language games' and will sometimes speak of a primitive language as a 'language game.'

This statement heralds one of the major points of departure from the direction outlined in the *Tractatus*. Wittgenstein's shift in thinking between the *Tractatus* and *Investigations* aligns with the general shift in 20th century philosophy from analytic and logical positivism to behaviourism and then pragmatism. It is a conceptual shift from seeing language as a fixed structure imposed upon the world, to seeing it as fluid and flexible that is connected to the inventiveness of everyday life, for everyone. Culture must be central to this idea. The later or new Wittgenstein, creating meaningful statements is not a matter of mapping the logical form of the world, it is a matter of using regular and/or colloquial expressions within the new term of 'language games' that are played and understood by adults and children alike. He proclaimed that 'In most cases, the meaning of a word is its use.' From this position, it is possible to understand Wittgenstein's general view of mathematics, perhaps paraphrased as 'In most cases, the meaning of mathematics is its use.' For example, Ernest (1998, p. 75) suggests that 'Wittgenstein proposed a naturalistic and fallibilist social philosophy of mathematics. The naturalism relates to his attachment to descriptive philosophy which gives priority to mathematical practice.' Ernest goes on to state that Wittgenstein (1978, p. 38) 'repudiates the notion that mathematics needs or derives any security from its "foundations"'

> What does mathematics need a foundation for? It no more needs one, I believe, than propositions about physical objects – or about sense impressions need an analysis. What mathematical propositions do stand in need of is clarification of their grammar, just as do those other propositions.
>
> The mathematical problems of what is called foundations are no more the foundations of mathematics for us than the painted rock is the support of the painted tower.

Debate regarding Wittgenstein's approach to philosophy and to the philosophy of mathematics will continue, with vigour, as it should. What this shows however is that there are different ways of viewing mathematics and that the common and conservative approach to school mathematics followed my many countries of the world, can be contested. A culturally-responsive, practice-based, integrated knowledge and inquiry learning approach to school mathematics is equally defensible. Taking Indigenous and non-Indigenous social and community practices as the starting point, can form the basis of a new form of mathematical knowledge for all children that conceptualises school mathematics as a philosophical field of cultural practice, in the same way that other fields of practice constitute the school curriculum. Schools as we know them are then taken in the opposite direction. Mathematics, like arts and other knowledges, suggest more than we can know, drawing us into knowledge, personal knowledge that cannot be quantified about the world, but is part of us just the same.

4   Excursus 4: Rock Pools

Reaching down into the cold, crystal-clear salt water, I disturbed a rock on the bottom to see what was revealed underneath. On this occasion, a small crab scurried about, indignant at having its morning interrupted, attempting to burrow into the sand. I reached down and placed a mixture of sand and crab on the palm of my hand. My new friend was quite small, no more than two or three centimetre across with, as far as I could see, eight legs and tiny pincers at the front. It was a motley green colour and I could feel its crusty skin or skeleton as it scrambled about on my hand. For some reason, I thought about the crayfish that came off the boats each morning when they returned to port, much larger of course, but red-orange with many legs and claws that could give you a nasty nip if you weren't careful. I gently placed the crab back in the rock pool and placed the stone I had dislodged nearby. This ritual was part of my usual routine, if not every day, then certainly every weekend, whatever the weather, when I could explore along the coastline to my heart's content. There was something inherently interesting about waiting for low tide and to see what had been left behind on the rock shelf. There were usually pieces of green and brown seaweed and kelp, various creatures within shells of fascinating shapes and type, small fish darting about glinting in the sunshine and sea anemone, like marine spikey flowers that would close when you placed your finger inside. Foreign invaders beware! We grew up being warned about the blue ringed octopus, again small in stature, but poisonous at the same time, sometimes angry and trapped in the rock pools. As I moved carefully on the rough and slippery sandstone of the shelf under my feet, my mind wandered to the collection of shells I had found when running along the dunes away from the main beach. Our teacher had told us about how the local Aboriginal people who had lived in this area many years ago, would live in part on food from the sea and when finished, would throw their used shells and bones from crabs, mussels and fish onto a pile. Over time, as the wind covered the shells with sand, a *midden* would be created, a semi-permanent reminder of those who had gone before. I had never told anyone of my discovery and as far as I could recall, had never heard other members of my beach-going family tell similar stories. I wondered if Aboriginal children had clambered over these age-old rocks as well, like me, for many centuries, exploring the pools for what they held, examples of life in many forms and objects of curiosity and imagination. What stories had their parents told them? Perhaps I would go fishing later.

CHAPTER 5

Language Connections with the World

> Let no-one say the past is dead, the past is all about us and within.
> OODGEROO NOONUCCAL

∵

Greek, European, American and Indigenous philosophy have provided historical and cultural guidance for considering Indigenous and non-Indigenous knowledge arising from dialectical processes as different situations interact and design the new. Current experience becomes entangled with previous understandings to create new perceptions of social reality. Grammars of language that exist in the brain enable such connections to be made, ultimately causing thought, speech and then communication between participants. This chapter discusses a descriptive, non-technical approach to the centrality of language for learning and suggests a dialectical process of language and knowledge meaning. The principle of 'discursiveness' is raised as a 'way of thinking about' Indigenous curriculum.

1   Formations of Society, Language, Thought

Children from all families around the world regardless of socio-economic and geographical background, should have the right to schooling that is respectful of the right to know and consequently the right to learn. This involves access to the most valued knowledge of each society together with the opportunity and encouragement to construct new personal understandings based on investigation, critical analysis and educational discourse. For Indigenous communities and particularly those who live within the stultifying dominance of neoliberal economics, public schooling has generally not provided such occasions given the intractability of recognising Indigenous knowledge, culture and language. From an international perspective, in countries such as Australia, New Zealand, Canada and the United States, any discussion on Indigenous languages needs to recognise the existence of diversity or homogeneity of language and should be presented in the historical context of suppression under the regime of missions, reserves and boarding schools. During the Aboriginal Protectorate era in Australia (circa 1838–1969; similar to Indian Agents in United States and Canada), Aboriginal people were not allowed to speak language or practice culture which, in some regions, led to the language effectively dying out. Loss of language means that survival of Indigenous humanity is at stake (May & Hill, 2018; Reyhner & Eder, 2017). Policy and practice in many countries for preservation, maintenance and revitalisation of Indigenous languages should be a national priority involving capability building for every community in strengthening its local language and enabling all citizens to participate with language as well. From a philosophical and pragmatist viewpoint, knowledge, culture and language are in constant interrelationship and the suppression of one repudiates the others. For example, the Soviet psychologist and linguist Vygotsky (1896–1934) noted in a most remarkable statement (Vygotsky, 1978, p. 24):

> The most significant moment in the course of intellectual development, which gives birth to the purely human forms of practical and abstract intelligence, occurs when speech and practical activity, two previously completely independent lines of development, converge.

In the space of a few lines, Vygotsky describes the basis of being human. He states that 'purely human forms of practical and abstract intelligence,' or how humans think in a manner quite distinct from other living species – the issue of theory and practice, or concrete and abstract thought raised previously – happens when 'speech and practical activity' become as one, as the regular process of engaging the world continues. Vygotsky calls this, 'The most significant moment in the course of intellectual development,' an unqualified claim for all people in relation to age, culture, or economic status. He goes on to discuss how involvement with the social and physical environment, generates human speech and that this not only changes the child or person, but also changes the environment itself, so that there is constant movement or transformation between them. A young child for example, with a small vocabulary at that age, may be playing with a dog and reaches out to stroke its fur. In response, the dog may lift its paw for the child to hold. At that moment, the child appreciates the dog in a way that was not possible a few seconds before. Tentative and new thoughts occur in the brain as a result of new sensory perceptions that changes the meaning of 'dog' for the child, or any learner. Vygotsky (1978) summarises this situation by observing that for children, 'their speech and action are part of one and the same complex psychological function, directed towards the solution of the problem at hand' (p. 25). This is a pragmatist explanation, as encountered in the previous chapter.

In a similar manner to Vygotsky, the American linguist and philosopher, Noam Chomsky (1928–) theorised the connections between human activity, thought and speech. In the mid-1950s, Chomsky opposed the current behaviourist view of language acquisition whereby children developed language through the external and passive provision of information and reinforcement. Instead, Chomsky proposed in controversial fashion that all humans had an internal 'disposition' or 'faculty' for language, suggesting that all languages had the same innate structure, or universal grammar, not imposed from throughout. The use of the generic term 'grammar' can be somewhat misleading, in that Chomsky is referring here to how the brain as a biological organ functions, rather than the rules and conventions of written and spoken speech that have been decided by humans. He contributes a general description of this approach in the following way (Chomsky, 1979, p. 36):

> The theory of language is simply that part of human psychology that is concerned with one particular 'mental organ,' human language. Stimulated by appropriate and continuing experience, the language faculty creates a grammar that generates sentences with formal and semantic properties. We say that a person knows the language generated by this grammar.

This view of language can be considered as 'matter of fact' in that there is an inherent human quality called *language,* in the same way as other qualities are called *sight*, *breathing* and *motion*. Whether there is a separate 'mental organ' for language production, or whether language like consciousness are qualities that arise from molecular arrangements of human being, is still subject to philosophical debate. It should be noted that Chomsky supports Vygotsky in that language is 'stimulated by appropriate and continuing experience' such that thoughts produced in the brain can ultimately be expressed as speech. It may be necessary to think of two types of language: firstly, an internal mechanism generated in the brain from which thoughts occur and secondly, the production of speech that enables an external relationship with the environment to be established. With this understanding, language can be thought of as an act, that enables the next act. Figure 3 depicts this arrangement.

What is suggested here is that a fabric of acts is constantly being undertaken by each human as they progress through the day. There is action taken on an object of interest including physical problems to be overcome, ideas to be considered and interests to be satisfied. In Vygotskian terms, this process is called the 'object-motive act,' where we act on objects to seek meaning. Within the context of the social act, defined by Mead (Gillespie, 2005) as a collective

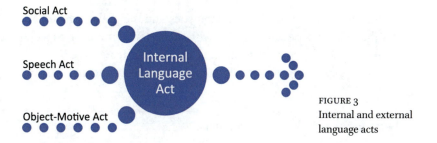

FIGURE 3
Internal and external language acts

act involving collective meaning for participants, thought is constructed and speech acts become possible.

The significance of Vygotsky and Chomsky for educators while not necessarily agreeing with all their insights, is that both have provided a progressive way of thinking about what it means to be human regarding knowledge, culture and language. These are respectful considerations for all people, Indigenous and non-Indigenous alike. Indigenous peoples see their languages as being unique and has been an extension of their relationship to the land. As such language reclamation in Indigenous communities is a constant act of rebellion and resistance, and also as a marker that sets aside Indigenous students and their communities from the destructive theories of national cohesion and multiculturalism. To reiterate, the human organism has a disposition for language, in the same way that it is set up for two feet, a nervous system and blood circulation. We can think of how the brain works as a grammar, similar to how the universe works because of the nature of the universe itself, not dependent on human rules and symbols based on our observations. This grammar, or what is called 'mentalese' or the 'language of thought' has syntax and semantics or 'mental states' that enables it to produce thought. It exists at a level 'below' that of what we verbalise, likened to the hidden machine code of a computer that operates to produce an output. However we are still at the position of trying to generalise models of thought that can be criticised by another descriptive model, opening up the question of what lies at the most fundamental level, there can always be something else lying in wait for different understanding. There are two reasons why these are important matters for teachers. In the first instance, the notion of a 'language of thought,' opens up our view of all students before us in every class. There is a broader view of human complexity and what each student might be thinking regardless of what the teacher believes students should be thinking – and how. Secondly, the language of thought suggests mental states in the brain that connect with external experience, necessitating an emphasis on social practice as the basis of human inquiry, rather than only pre-existing cognitive architecture itself. How these representations are formed and exist is another matter. While it continues to be uncertain, excitedly so, linguistics and the philosophy of language show that teachers are not mere conduits of content with passive receivers. They are instead the neurotransmitters of learning for each and every student who sits before them, replete with personal curiosity and imagination.

2 Perspective of Indigenous Language

Considering language as an act that enables the next act, has significant implications for how human conversation, communication and the development, sharing and contestation of viewpoints are perceived. This is not the only understanding of language as intense debate around the world on literacy and numeracy attests. Formal schooling tends to concentrate on the structure of spoken and written language rather than emphasising the social and cultural context within which language is generated. This is particularly so for Indigenous peoples in minority positions. Battiste (2015, p. 142) comments on this problem when she writes:

> Every child born learns at least one language. In many countries, children learn many languages, both within their own families and in the local schools, making the norm not just bilingualism but multilingualism. This fact stands in marked contrast to the failure of education systems in the Western world to teach second or third languages.

Speaking about Aboriginal peoples in Canada, but the situation applies elsewhere, Battiste goes on to describe the many situations that regular schools and teachers can face. Students can be monolingual in an Aboriginal language, monolingual in English, bilingual in an Aboriginal language and English, or speak a combination of English and an Aboriginal language depending on the circumstances. It may also be the case that the family Indigenous language is not spoken completely at home such that the notion of bilingual is not entirely accurate. There are many problems to be overcome here regarding Indigenous and non-Indigenous qualified teachers in many languages, the incorporation of language across the curriculum and the use of language at home and in the community. Adopting a bilingual or multilingual approach across schooling systems is extraordinarily complex.

According to ShadowWalker (2019, p. 4), there is a marked contrast between Native American thinking as being community-based and spiral rather than one-dimensional in function and Western pedagogy which sees cognition as available to individuals through internal mental processes. ShadowWalker writes:

> This linear hierarchical thinking creates a power struggle and conflict for most American Indians since knowledge is appropriate through the social structure which is dependent on time and social participation for acquisition and mastery. The knowledge or internal mental processes are accessible through direct experience and observation within the community, family or home environment. The accessibility is not limited to the individual but is a dynamic analysis occurring with each interaction between the individual and society.

As has been noted above, there are significant differences within non-Indigenous philosophy on the composition of human thinking, but much similarity as well regarding the 'social participation' required for language construction. When ShadowWalker describes the connection between 'internal mental processes' and 'direct experience and observation' for Indigenous people, there is a strong relationship established with pragmatism in general and the role of knowledge and culture as envisioned by Vygotsky. In addition, the process of languaging occurs at once within the context of society for all learners including children and does not depend on a state of intellectual maturity being reached before specific acts of language become possible; there is a dialectical process at work involving the individual and society at all times, from birth. For Indigenous and non-Indigenous peoples, a further question is raised at this point regarding what is called 'linguistic pragmatics,' a field of study that looks at not only how meaning is communicated, but the social milieu as well in which the speaker and listener relate and their respective knowledge backgrounds. The culture and organisation of regular schooling is therefore clearly an important factor that impacts on all learning including language.

Worawa Aboriginal College recognises all languages spoken by the students and encourages the girls to use their first language while at school. In this way the College values 'the knowledge ... each individual brings to the learning situation' (Hooley, 2009, p. 69). Teachers at Worawa said:

> Recognition of language is recognition of culture and a recognition of the strengths that students bring with them to school. The students are free to speak in their language wherever, and whenever they like; whilst those who come without an Aboriginal language often learn from those who do. It is heartening to see some of the young students who have grown up speaking English, learning some of the languages of the other students.

Students at the College are representative of approximately 25 different language groups, with some students speaking up to three or four different languages or dialects, whilst others may only know a few words. Each week, the girls work together in their language groups on language enrichment activities. They have the opportunity to produce resources, or to research and learn more about their languages. They also participate in Yorta Yorta and Woiwarrung lessons with Aunty Zeta Thomson, as part of their Aboriginal Culture classes. Aboriginal Elder Nancy Djambutj from Milingimbi stated:

> I believe that strong language means strong learning and that means strong culture. I want all Aboriginal children to have strong language, strong learning and strong culture and to feel proud and confident about who they are as Aboriginal people.

Discussion of bi- and multilingualism and teaching a different language to speakers of other languages is beyond the scope of this book (see Javier, 2010). However we are aware that young children who are immersed in a culture of different languages can speak, communicate and find meaning in more than one language without formal teaching. This is the point made by Chomsky above regarding universal grammar. The notion of 'immersion schools' has been taken up in New Zealand (2008) where classes conducted in Maori have contributed to the maintenance and revitalisation of Indigenous language. It should be remembered that, 'During most of the last century, the use of Maori language in schools was actively discouraged, in order to promote instead assimilation of the Maori into European culture as rapidly as possible' (UN, 2006). Within Australia, about 16,000 Indigenous students and 13,000 non-Indigenous students located in 260 Australian schools are involved in an Indigenous language programme, with about 80 different Indigenous languages being taught. Overall, approximately 28 percent of programs are first language maintenance programs, about 12 percent are second language learning programs and about 50 percent are language retrieval programs (see Purdie et al., 2008). In a number of key principles that seem to apply across countries, the Australian report stated in part that language must only be taught by agreement with the Indigenous custodians, that 'learning an Indigenous language and becoming proficient in the English language are complementary rather than mutually exclusive activities' and that 'the most successful school language programmes will flow from a collaborative approach involving Indigenous communities, Indigenous Language Centres, linguists, schools and teachers' (pp. viii–ix). Further support for the fulsome participation of Indigenous peoples in regular schooling can be found in the concept of 'funds of knowledge' (Gonzalez, Moll, & Amanti, 2005), arising from research conducted with families on the border between the United States and Mexico and recognition of the knowledges and resources embedded in life experiences of local communities and classrooms. From these practices and limited examples, it seems clear that mainstream schooling around the world has made various attempts to assist the education of Indigenous families and children, together with the preservation of language, but many serious cultural and economic problems remain. A more philosophically robust and practice-based approach to integrated knowledge, culture and language is required.

In bringing together notions of history and culture, Vygotsky initially and colleagues in subsequent years developed an approach towards analysing human situations and the relationship between what people do and how they think. Known as Cultural Historical Activity Theory (CHAT), the process of thinking is seen to be mediated between the subject and object/s of experience, rather than there being a direct line of action with the social and physical worlds. For Vygotsky, tools, signs and especially language, were objects of mediation. This means that numerous interrelated factors need to be taken into account when considering how learning takes place, in contrast to the behaviourist approach that views the human subject responding directly to stimulus. In working with a number of schools in England on teacher education, Ellis (2011, p. 188) describes the cultural-historical approach as follows:

> A CHAT perspective on developing professional practice understands knowledge as accessed and developed in joint work on a potentially shared object. Consequently, knowledge is understood as existing as much among participants in the same field of practice as it does within them and that the creation of professional knowledge (at the level of concepts and patterns of social organisation) might take place in the transformation of the object of activity.

Ellis explains that knowledge occurs socially as groups consider 'shared objects' of their interest, such as cooking a meal, graphing the temperature of winter, or being told what to do by others. He gives the example of teachers (as subject) coming to a different understanding of how a class of students (as object) transforms when the number of students is decreased, making new procedures possible. The Finnish researcher Engeström (1999) further theorised CHAT as involving 'activity systems' that interact and produce deeper focus and awareness of the interrelationships between mediating rules, associated communities and how authority is distributed within the group. For example, a working party of teachers that is designing an innovative program for Indigenous and non-Indigenous children, will need to act within the requirements of the curriculum (rules), the views of parents including respect for language (communities) and how decisions are made (division of authority). The tensions and contradictions that exist between these factors cannot be ignored and will need to be analysed carefully so that overall progress and consensus can be accomplished. Curriculum and pedagogy that is appreciated in terms of cultural and historical factors in recognition that knowledge is co-produced between teachers, students and communities working together, offers a legitimate educational framework for Indigenous and non-Indigenous esteem. It may be of course, that the mediating factors mentioned above in any activity system, are confusing and difficult to accommodate. The resolution of common problems requires not only good will, but a comprehensive understanding of the political, economic and cultural forces that infuse social life and must be resolved with dexterity for mutual benefit.

3   Language of Visual Thought and Expression

Human thinking has sought to express itself in various ways since its beginning. This is a continuous process of acting in relation to the events of experience and of deciding what future acts are required to move forward. Customs that are categorised as 'the arts' including dance, music, drama, visual formats and the like require a thorough discussion in relation to language and ideas, but will be restricted to consideration of visual practices here. In terms of visual expression and its history, we are aware of Indigenous rock art that can be observed in various countries such as Spain, Indonesia and Australia. Such art is very old and was painted long before the development of oral language as it is known today. This prompts the question of why rock art was considered necessary at the time, what was intended to convey and what significance can be placed on the images and symbols used? For the people concerned, we can envisage procedures of acting, thinking, changing and acting again as drawing continued. It may be that the actual thinking of all participants is uncertain and difficult to reveal, but the products of visual artistic endeavour do give some indication of human thought. Language does the same.

Painting in various styles today is used to continue the cultural stories handed down by Elders and the important knowledge of country and community events of Indigenous peoples. As well as cultural significance, Martineau and Ristkes (2014, p. 11) suggest that:

> Indigenous art reclaims and revitalizes the inherent creative potentiality of art to be activated in political struggle, not as an inseparable aesthetic experience but embedded in the embodied daily life experience of Indigenous peoples, settlers and others globally.

Connecting the political with the aesthetic would be the intention of many artists and indeed, is difficult to prevent. Painting of the landscape from an Indigenous perspective for example may quite conceivably raise discussion of land rights. The water colour paintings of the ancient and desert areas of central Australia by Indigenous Australian Albert Namatjira during the 1940s and 1950s made many people aware of the inland regions of the country for the first time and the need to be respectful of the physical environment. Such light and colour, such unknown beauty and uniqueness! Indigenous children in school today will be acutely aware of their responsibility in maintaining cultural habits, history and ethics and the role of art as an important strategy.

Human growth and world view are not only connected to the past, for action in the present, but are linked to a changed and/or better future. Such a future cannot be accurately predicted, meaning that there is always a tension between the sum total of experience to this point and what might follow. Art can have this characteristic as well, with the artist and connoisseur making judgement about the artefact, but the impact of its presence in the world remains to be seen, perhaps now or later. Artistic expression today can be interpreted in aesthetic and epistemological terms. That is, while art in all its forms generates enjoyment and a sense of fulfillment, it also produces new thinking about the issues depicted both for the artist and for the spectator. The act of producing each piece brings into being new understandings as the work unfolds and new thoughts of interpretation as different eyes are brought to bear. For example, we may have some idea of what Monet was thinking when he looked out his Paris window and noted the murky, grimy atmosphere and the reddish sun, resulting in his painting 'Impression, Sunrise.' Again, it is possible to surmise what was in Picasso's mind when he painted 'Guernica,' showing the horror of war and the fascist bombing of a Spanish village, but do we really know? In each case, we have the thinking of the artist displayed and the thinking of the observer created.

For its part, the public accepts such art as knowledge, culture and language. For Aboriginal people, art connects with history, culture, their sense of identity and self-concept; important themes in life are narrated through art, themes that shape past, present and future living. Through art people are connected to their specific community. Significant too is the ability of artistic expression to enable the artist to discover inner resources that engender resilience in both the individual and community. Davis understands involvement in art to be especially significant in Australia as Australian Aboriginal people are striving to 'reclaim their cultural identity' (Davis et al., 2001, p. 3). In art, both traditional and contemporary Aboriginal culture are expressed, and she considers 'they would provide an excellent tool for bridging the gap between how Aboriginal people used to live and how they need to live now' (p. 3). All students then need to have the educational opportunity of exploring their cultural heritage and understanding through visual media and to make their imaginations, interpretations and values available for public exposure and challenge strengthening Indigenous and non-Indigenous definition in the process.

4 Reflective Interlude

At this point and before proceeding, we need to reflect on the discussion so far and the key issues that have been raised for Indigenous and non-Indigenous education. Chapter 1 began with the assertion from the United Nations that 'Traditional knowledge is at the core of Indigenous identity, culture and heritage around the world' and that the difficult struggle for cultural continuance and rejuvenation takes place within the restrictions of global neoliberalism. Strategies to combat neoliberal influence in education need to be devised. Chapter 2 considered the experience of Indigenous students at Worawa Aboriginal College, Australia and their efforts at maintaining and strengthening Indigeneity and compassionate humanity. Key features of the Worawa curriculum were identified and further detailed in further chapters. Chapters 3, 4 and 5 above have taken up the dialectical questions of knowledge, culture and language and how these characteristics of being human are shared around the world under different economic circumstances. Oral, written and communicative language in particular was identified as central for constructing and expressing our humanity and in a pragmatist sense, was described in terms of 'language as act, to enable the next act.'

Based on these considerations Chapter 6 will take up discussion regarding education as 'philosophy of practice' and suggested that the philosophy of pragmatism and praxis was an appropriate way of framing the integration of theory and practice in daily and professional life. Praxis is taken from the Greek notion of the action and judgements required for a life well-lived.

In general terms, these chapters have attempted to briefly outline the main issues of an explicit and progressive philosophy of education that is currently lacking in many countries, a philosophy that focuses on human practice arising from social and cultural experience and the discussion and theorising of that practice amongst participants: the prudent activity and wisdom of ordinary people. Discussion so far has emphasised an open forum or dialogue, a 'way of thinking' about formal education that is accessible for Indigenous families and children and that brings Indigenous and non-Indigenous knowledge and understandings together wherever possible (see Alaska Native Knowledge

Network for approach and resources regarding integrated learning [ANKN], 2020). Each community needs to develop its own way of living and educating to meet its own aspirations. For example, a draft proposal for 'discursive curriculum' has therefore been suggested as a means of combining these ideas for schools whatever their population or location. Major Indigenous and non-Indigenous authors and theorists referenced above are linked by their support for human action and inquiry and how knowledge occurs through the interrelationship between experience and thought. They oppose conservative behaviourist viewpoints where humans are seen as passive receivers of information, knowledge and instruction already known by others. These theorists and writers have historical stature and their views are congruent with Indigenous philosophy of holistic existence involving ceremony, culture, land and community, enabling knowledge and stories in their own words. There is much commonality at the 'practice interface' between peoples.

5   Excursus 5: A Process of Eyes Opened Wide

Growing up in a medium-sized country town can limit your opportunities when it comes to education after school. Other members of the family were working in local factories, but I had a feeling of wanting to know more. Reading was a personal enjoyment whether tales of schoolboy adventures in England, stories of lands across the seas, or poems about the bush and explorers. For some reason, I decided to enrol in a Diploma of Chemistry, probably because of my love for the outdoors and the connections I felt with the nearby environment, the ocean, rivers and animals that I visited almost on a daily basis. Science was a way of getting closer to the natural world. It soon became clear that doing experiments in senior chemistry struck a chord in my mind, particularly as they seemed to be drawing me in to what was happening, in a different way to the few activities we had undertaken in our junior science classes. There the answers were known by the teacher and it was all too mechanical. I became fascinated with trying to work out what I observed to satisfy my own curiosity, I wanted detailed explanation: exactly why did each salt burn with a different colour, why were some substances acidic and others alkaline, what were magnetic lines of force, how is it possible to extract chlorophyll from various plants? We were a small group of diploma students who had similar interests in what we were learning and the relationship with our teachers was friendly and respectful. Our discussions about the nature of the universe were exciting. It was late one afternoon in the lab and we were getting ready to leave when, after commenting on my results, Mr Johnson happened to mention quietly,

'Have you ever thought of going to university?' This surprised me enormously, a completely new thought that had never entered my head before. Not only had this never been mentioned in my family – it was something that no-one ever contemplated – but it was not a topic of conversation in the local town as well, of leaving home to go to university in the big city. As a shy country boy, I'm still not sure how I made the transition, but with Mr Johnson's and my nervous and somewhat uncertain family's support, I began the next stage of my journey into chemistry and indeed, the big wide world itself. I have often wondered what might have occurred if those words of 'Have you ever thought of going to university?' had not echoed around my brain, at that time, in those circumstances, in the chemistry lab. Perhaps I was ready to hear them.

CHAPTER 6

Education as Philosophy of Pragmatism and Practice

> You may write me down in history / With your bitter, twisted lies /
> You may trod me in the very dirt / But still, like dust, I'll rise.
> MAYA ANGELOU

∴

Analysing education as philosophy of practice, the problem of integrating practice and theory across all levels of education remains a major impediment to the development of personal meaning. Knowledge occurs when events need to be resolved for personal and mutual interest and the impact of human acts can be observed. Abstracting general ideas from social action and thinking about what is abstract in concrete terms, is a significant human achievement that may not be present in formal education. This chapter discusses how American Pragmatism has conceptualised these dilemmas and provides guidance for practitioners. It is suggested that the philosophy of pragmatism offers an appropriate framework for Indigenous education and can be incorporated for the education of all learners. The philosophy of pragmatism is not being imposed on Indigenous learning, but is a way of thinking about Indigenous knowing and philosophy for application in formal education at all levels.

1   Coming to Practice

Following the conclusion at the end of Chapter 2 imaginative combinations of the 'Worawa Way,' portfolios, knowledge exemplars and commitment to peace and justice would be facilitated by the adoption of signature pedagogies of pragmatist application. The notion of 'signature' is taken to mean essential and significant characteristics that define and authorise an issue and 'pedagogy' as the broad strategy adopted to investigate human practice. The eight signature pedagogies (Table 3) clearly authorise human practice, praxis and the central concerns of pragmatism, that is integrated knowledge and inquiry learning.

TABLE 3   Signature pedagogies of pragmatist application

Signature pedagogies	Characteristics of signature pedagogies			
Professional practice	Recognises personal learning from immersion in practice	Positions participant interest as central concern without bias	Supports communities of practice to support inquiry for improved learning environments and student learning	Continuing critique of practice for change of conditions to formulate ideas of new practice
Repertoire of practice	Identifies and articulates features of pedagogical, curriculum, assessment practices	Adopts mix of innovative practices to meet specific needs	Links key features of pedagogy, curriculum, assessment for change and improvement	Critiques repertoires of educational practice as social activity that supports satisfaction and progress
Teacher as researcher	Systematically investigates own practice for improvement	Recognises research as situated in participant experience	Participates as member of school-based research team/s	Relates local, national and global research, policy and practice
Case conferencing	Generates case and commentary writing for understanding of practice	Authorises narration and commentary of lifeworld case and story	Participates in case conferencing and concept analysis for production of teachers' knowledge	Encourages articulation and analysis of teachers' knowledge in relation to theories of curriculum and teaching
Community partnership	Connects with local communities	Ensures partner relationships are 'without prejudice'	Integrates community culture and knowledge into curriculum	Investigates community to understand local aspiration, history, knowledge, language

(*cont.*)

TABLE 3 Signature pedagogies of pragmatist application (*cont.*)

Signature pedagogies	Characteristics of signature pedagogies			
Praxis learning	Investigates/ provides description, explanation, theorising and change of practice in response to reflective practice	Supports autonomous, non-coercive practices	Demonstrates a curriculum developed from praxis and in response to reflection	Constructs learning environments of ethically-informed action for the public good
Participatory action research	Identifies and advocates key issues of policy and participates in collecting data for analysis	Encourages participation of all cultural backgrounds	Contributes to project discourses with internal and external team members	Theorises and critiques research findings in the public domain
Portfolio dialogue	Compiles and discusses artefacts of personal learning over time	Assists new praxis through problematising experience, themes and actions	Participates with artefacts and knowledge discourses that show understandings of meanings of practice	Demonstrates a coherent philosophy consistent with personalised practice and community change for public good

They recognise the role of each participant as researcher and co-producer of knowledge through strategies such as case writing and conferencing and working in partnership with community-based teams of investigators. Democratic dialogue is encouraged through negotiated projects and the compilation of portfolios of artefacts that show personal thinking over time. Issues of equity, ethical conduct and indeed power relationships are considered through practices that involve judgement, decision-making and grappling with knowledge and procedures that can seek to dominate, rather than respectfully include diverse viewpoints. Taken as a whole, the eight signature pedagogies give rise to a comprehensive and critical approach not only to knowledge, but to society as well and therefore consideration of the range of features that impinge on any social situation. For schooling, curriculum and teaching, this means that current knowledge informs and that new knowledge is created, becoming evident from experience, the culture, histories and language of people as they engage in transforming their worlds for the better. The signature pedagogies as envisaged have emancipatory intent, negating forms of oppression, discrimination and marginalisation that are found in unequal societies and institutions.

Systems of formal education around the world have difficulty in bringing theory and practice together at all year levels and for all topics. This is because explicit definitions of theory and practice are often not agreed either philosophically or by the education profession of a particular country in relation to student learning and how they impact on different approaches to teaching and curriculum. In broad terms, the notion of theory (Greek: *theoria*; observing, contemplating) relates to general propositions and understandings that explain phenomena and guide actions, whereas practice involves the application of ideas and processes to achieve a particular end. From this, it can be seen that theory and practice are intimately connected, occurring simultaneously, without one there is not the other. In proposing his theory of cognitive development, for example, the Swiss epistemologist Piaget (Marti & Rodreguez, 2015) suggested a concrete operational stage for young children and a formal operational stage for older children and young adults. For the learner, a concrete object has identifiable features of existence such as texture, weight and colour, while a formal or abstract object is removed from direct experience and exists as concepts in the mind only. A key strategy for teaching when students are confronting a new idea, is to 'make the formal or abstract, concrete,' so that connections can be made between what is already known and what is yet to be known. Making the formal or abstract concrete can be interpreted as integrating theory and practice for all learning across the curriculum, or alternatively, if theory and practice are not integrated, then learning is severely inhibited, if not denied.

A further way of thinking about how to enact the integration of theory and practice, is provided by the Brazilian educator and theorist, Freire and his concept of dialogue. He describes dialogue as 'the encounter of those addressed to the common task of learning and acting' (Freire, 2014, p. 88). The essence of dialogue is the word, conceived as having two constituents 'reflection and action, in such radical interaction that if one is sacrificed – even in part – the other immediately suffers' (p. 87). Freire comments that dialogue consisting of trust, humility and critical thinking is necessary to transform the world where thinking and learning are always in a dynamic relationship with acting and doing. Dialogue conducted in this way between participants who are interested in understanding a situation and changing it for mutual benefit, produces 'generative themes' of conversation regarding the situation and its main areas of importance. A group of residents for instance, in discussing how to reclaim an old and disused industrial site for a community park, will need to consider the history of the site, talk with local Indigenous peoples regarding cultural significance, carefully plan the type and number of trees and shrubs to be planted and foster environmental arguments in relation to proposals for residential development. Arising from these discussions, generative themes will structure principles and key ideas regarding the purpose of the park, such as the need for green wedges within cities, the combination of industrial and public spaces, employment opportunities, provision for family recreation and for schools to conduct outdoor curriculum activities. Community members have been involved in an overall process of dialogue that consists of community interest, problem-posing about that interest, production of generative themes through discussion, identifying avenues to problem-solving and finally, taking action to move their project forward. At the heart of Freire's dialogical approach to making the world a better place is the notion of the interrelationship between theory and practice and how what we might call 'practice-theorising' constitutes daily living. A summary and generative theme of integrated knowledge and inquiry learning therefore seems appropriate for regular schooling.

The historic question now arises regarding exactly why the combination of theory and practice has been extremely difficult to achieve in formal education at all levels and why the recognised approaches of researchers and authors such as Piaget and Freire have not become more mainstream. These are generalisations despite the committed and determined work of progressive educators around the world. As mentioned in Chapter 1, our starting point must be the neoliberal economic context and how this has influenced curriculum and teaching (Apple, 2006). In noting that 'curriculum is the course of experience/s that forms human beings into persons,' Ball (2012, p. 30) also goes on to write that:

> The 'curriculum' here is about the public sector learning to confront its purported inadequacies, learning lessons from the methods and values of the private sector and learning to reform itself. As well as in another sense, learning the 'hard lessons; taught by the disciplines of the market. All of this involves the instilling of new sensibilities and values and new forces of social relations, into the practices of the public sector.

In this segment, Ball includes regular education as an aspect of the neoliberal economy that must be reformed along the lines of market imperatives. This may be an intention, but very difficult to achieve without a comprehensive program of reform, based on what might be called neoliberal educational philosophy. Market forces usually refer to supply and demand for goods and services and competition between commodities that set quality, price and availability. Based on these ideas, Hooley (2012, p. 25) has summarised the features of neoliberal epistemology as a guide to their application (Table 4). These features emphasise a disorderly approach towards learning with a belief that not all can achieve, some will grow and become strong, while others will wither and become intellectually bankrupt. A neoliberal epistemology that is true to these principles will most likely adopt a non-regulatory or laissez-faire approach to schooling teaching and learning where neither conservative nor liberal achievement is paramount, but the fact that some will progress more and others less, the natural order of things. Despite neoliberal dominance, this will be difficult to achieve as matters of public policy in those societies where community expectations of its schooling system are high and includes strengthening values of educational equity, socially significant content and responsible citizenship. Bringing theory and practice together in all learning should characterise such expectation.

2   Background to Pragmatism and Pragmatists

All ideas are the products of their age. Some ideas persist, perhaps for centuries, while others are refined or dispatched. The notion of democracy for example seems to be significant and has endured since the Greeks, whereas alchemy does not appear to be useful. During the period of European Enlightenment, the industrial revolution and the development of modern science and

TABLE 4   Summary features of neoliberal epistemology

Intersubjective practice	Little interest in specific philosophy regarding learning, consciousness, values norms; only outcomes by participants
Concrete, everyday knowledge	Individual-centred; diverse; active/passive; individual considerations; varied outcomes
Abstract, systematic knowledge	Student-based; disparate; active/passive; individual considerations; varied outcomes
Social justice impact	Rearranges personal and social hierarchies and relationships due to non-regulated individual capabilities.

technology, many advances have been made regarding our understanding of the universe and how to envision, design, make and incorporate processes and devices to assist contemporary living. That is, to put ideas into action. Philosophical ideas during this time developed and changed as well, with some major differences occurring between European or Continental Philosophy and American Philosophy. Following the American Civil War (1861–1865), the period between 1890 and 1920 became known as the Progressive Era, a time of social anxiety and activism regarding rapid development of the American republic involving industrialisation, urbanisation and mass immigration. Internationally, this period also includes World War I and the Russian Revolution that signalled major fractures with the past. Such dramatic events and rapid change had inevitable problems and consequences of economic boom and bust that spawned demands for reform, democratic process and peace. It is within this energetic context, that American Philosophy evolved, a period of new ideas, of substantial change and reform, of social and scientific development and of hope for creating a better future for the republic and its people. As a significant social practice, education was part of the progressive or reform movement, with public schools of the day where they were available being overcrowded, with poor facilities, exercising corporal punishment, little or no scope for student play and experiment and with limited teacher preparation. The time was ripe for a progressive educational philosophy to emerge.

In 1878, the American logician, writer and teacher, Charles Sanders Peirce (1839–1914) published his seminal paper entitled 'How To Make Our Ideas Clear,' in which he discussed the nature of thought and logic. He attempted to include the emerging scientific approach into philosophy and argued that meaning arises from empirical observation. This was in strong opposition to other viewpoints where questions such as what it means to be human, the nature of self and the origins of knowledge are mainly metaphysical and do not depend on the social practice of people. His paper set out to show how human ideas are based on our sense experience and that our idea of any thing or object depends on the effects that thing or object has on our sensibilities. Peirce wrote about the clarification of human ideas in the following manner (Peirce, 1955/2015a, p. 31):

> Consider what effects, that might conceivably have practical bearings, we conceive the object of our conception to have. Then, our conception of these effects is the whole of our conception of the object.

This statement by Peirce is taken to be the initiating moment of pragmatism (Greek: *pragma*; action, movement). He is not only saying how we come to understand ourselves, but how we make our thoughts and ideas clear for those with whom we live and work. In other words, we forge our relationship with the world through a pragmatist process of action, reflection, clarification and discourse. For example, in playing a game of tennis, we observe how the ball hits and bounces from the racquet and how and where it travels across the court, depending on the angle of the strings and where the face of the racquet is pointed. Experience is gained about the game of tennis, but also about the nature of force and the relationship between physical objects. We note the total effects of the ball and come to understand the concept of ball itself. In a further paper, Peirce recognises some clumsiness and confusion with the word 'pragmatism' and instead, 'begs to announce the birth of the word "pragmaticism," which is ugly enough to be safe from kidnappers' (Peirce, 1955/2015b, p. 255). Needless to say, his invention did not survive.

William James (1842–1910) was an American philosopher and psychologist who continued and developed the work of Peirce, making pragmatism very well-known particularly in an 1898 lecture. He came to view pragmatism as not only clarifying ideas and enabling meaning, but as a theory of truth. In an early piece, he commented that 'the knower is not merely a mirror floating with no foothold anywhere' (James, 1982, p. 125) and went on to state:

> The knower is an actor and coefficient of the truth on one side, whilst on the other, he registers the truth which he helps to create. Mental interests, hypotheses, postulates, so far as they are bases for human action – action which, to a great extent transforms the world – help to make the truth which they declare.

It is apparent that James connects thinking with changing the world and that ultimately, providing avenues to truth will be discerned. This may seem to be a big leap and controversial for its time, or any time. However it does demonstrate the necessity of pragmatism not only being concerned with actions that change the immediate, but actions that connect with the great ideas and problems of humanity. James draws a distinction between reality and truth such that mind induces truth upon reality. That is, we may accept a tree as being real, of existing, but our understanding of tree comes from our experience of it, in all its forms of growth across the seasons. Tracing the application of action over time leads to generation of the good, of life that progresses towards more humane existence.

John Dewey (1859–1952) believed that philosophy should not be remote and obscure, but be concerned with understanding and interacting with the problems of the day. He opposed dualisms and constantly sought to see the connectedness within and between phenomena, both social and physical. Drawing on the American republican experience of the time, it was Dewey who contrasted 'traditional' education (passive, teacher-dominated, set content) with 'progressive' education (active, student-centred, open content). In particular, Dewey emphasised the centrality of human action in creating sense and thought, recognising that thinking and action go together. He wrote extensively on a pragmatist approach to education in terms of integrated knowledge and inquiry learning. His view of democratic life as 'a form of associated living, of conjoint communicated experience' (Dewey, 1916, p. 87) can not only be taken as referring to relations between people, but as an expression of how the human biological organism functions. This is a fundamental principle for progressive educators. It shows that all humans at all times connect with their social and physical environments, combine their previous knowledge with current experience to produce new thought that in effect changes their environment and utilise their emergent dispositions to implement new actions. This is the formation of new knowledge. In this respect, Dewey's ideas were closely aligned with those of his colleague George Herbert Mead (1863–1931). In raising the concept of 'social act,' Mead postulated that human thought occurs through its connections with society, that is, form the outside in, rather than being pre-existent in the brain that then interacts with the environment. Again, biology and sociality, or mind and body, come together, each influencing and changing the other.

It is interesting to note that Dewey and Mead worked closely in Chicago with their colleague, Jane Addams (1860–1935). Addams was the founder and co-ordinator of Hull House, a refugee or settlement residence for destitute families, especially mothers and children. Dewey often visited Hull House where there were pragmatist principles of education and learning being developed, in the same way as he encouraged at the primary schools he established at the University of Chicago. Jane Addams was also a strong advocate for peace and stridently opposed American involvement in World War I. She was awarded the Nobel Prize for Peace in 1931. The American Pragmatists therefore – Peirce, James, Dewey, Mead and Addams – were not only responsible for proposing, developing and defending a new and progressive approach to philosophy, but they located philosophy, thought and knowledge within the broad sweep of human history, as something that all humans do as a result of being human, as a result of acting-thinking species being. Pragmatism needed to be associated with and explain the great human perplexities of the nature of existence.

3   Practice, Praxis and Signature Pedagogies

Extending the view of practice to that of the Greek concept of praxis, introduces the notion of practices that are intended to support living well, of human flourishing and satisfaction within social contexts, difficult and otherwise. Praxis can be thought of as the ongoing combination of theory and practice for change and improvement, the idea of practice-theorising, or more broadly, as involving major transformations in the historical, political and cultural realms (Kemmis & Smith, 2008). For educational purposes, praxis deepens our understanding of pragmatism and ensures that social and ethical concerns are incorporated into strategies for schooling, teaching and learning. It is then possible to develop a set of signature pedagogies (Hooley, 2018, pp. 53–54) to guide personal action and judgements for schooling and within specific circumstances for community well-being (Table 3). Programs underpinned by principles of this type, allow meaning to emerge from social acts rather than be imposed from throughout and to be actively constructed over short or long periods of time by consensus or agreement. The process is inherently equitable because it respects the culture and backgrounds of participants and the validity of their viewpoints. It should be noted that the suggested signature pedagogies do not establish a set of rules to be followed, but constitute a non-hierarchical framework of means of acting and thinking within educational and social settings. All horizontal cells of the table are of equal importance and are not arranged in order of difficulty from left to right.

A further way of thinking about the signature pedagogies and their application in total for peoples of different backgrounds, is through the concept of enactivism, closely related to constructivism and social practice. Enactivism is a theory of cognition emanating from an ecological paradigm. It is grounded in an analysis of living systems and cognition and emanates from a worldview as described by Macy (1983). It stems from the premise that 'cognition is a biological phenomenon and can only be understood as such' (Maturana & Varela, 1980, p. 7). Maturana and Varela describe knowing as 'effective action, that is, operating effectively in the domain of existence of living beings' (Maturana & Varela, 1992, p. 29). They maintain, 'cognition is effective action, an action that will enable a living being to continue its existence in a definite environment as it brings forth its world' (pp. 29–30). Cognition is not 'a representation of the world "out there," but rather an ongoing bringing forth of a world through the process of living itself' (p. 11). Knowledge, therefore, is effective behaviour in a given context, where the context is understood to be cultural in nature. Needless to say, such a conception of cognition and knowledge is at variance with the 'normal' understanding of these terms in schools. In her definition of learning, Hamilton (2005) includes an element of constructivism, in what is integrally an enactivist definition, following Begg (2000). She says:

> Learning is a complex co-emergent process of holistic development enabled through the construction of meaning, taking place within a community that is dynamic and robust in adapting to changing circumstances.

An exploration of enactivism would enable a re-thinking of the development of learning experiences that allows educators to develop practices that are theoretically consistent, and acknowledge learning as a complex web of interaction, where knowledge is understood as contingent, contextual and evolving; never absolute, universal or fixed. Freire (1973) described the antipathy of empowering learning as a monologue. Davis and Sumara (1997, p. 110) use the concept of conversation, when describing an enactivist theory of cognition. Davis and Sumara articulate four characteristics of conversational learning: The conversation:

1. leads the participants rather than they lead it
2. unfolds within the reciprocal, co-determined actions of the people involved
3. is a process of opening ourselves to others, at the same time as opening the possibility of affecting our understandings of the world
4. facilitates a movement towards consensus among persons whose thinking/acting can no longer be considered in strictly subjective terms.

A democratic classroom must be conversational in the manner described by Sumara. As noted previously, Dewey (1916, p. 87) says democracy 'is primarily a mode of associated living, of conjoint communicated experience.' If democracy is this, then it follows logically that a democratic classroom must be inclusive of all participants in a conversation about learning in a reciprocal, co-determined process. Hooley (ibid) relates the concept of a democratic classroom to Clendinnen's (2008) hope that Australian education because of the arrival of so many migrants from many different cultures, will become more and more inclusive. She hopes that Aboriginal learners will also be included, thus allowing the wider community to learn and value Aboriginal knowledge. Unfortunately, a key impediment to allowing this to occur in many schooling systems around the world, there remains a general lack of understanding assessment informing learning (see also Chapter 7), in particular of:

1. Assessment of learning (summative) to determine what the student has achieved,
2. Assessment for learning (formative) to inform the next stage of learning that will occur,
3. Ongoing assessment which focuses on teacher feedback alongside student reflection and self-assessment (assessment as learning: metacognition).

Rigour in education is applied to pedagogical approaches that encourage students to think critically, creatively, and more flexibly (Allen, 2012), expect students to learn at high levels, or a curriculum that is focused, coherent and appropriately challenging. Allen (ibid), reporting a conversation with Robyn Jackson, articulates four steps in rigorous learning. Learners need to:

1. know how to create their own meaning from their learning
2. organise information so they create mental models,
3. integrate individual skills into whole sets of processes, and then
4. apply what they have learned to new or novel situations.

Formative assessment is integral to this process as a teacher collects evidence of student understanding and leads them to further learning (Earl, 2003). Relevant is the derivation of the word education which means 'to draw out (*e-ducare*)' (Groome, 1998, p. 200, emphasis in original) and assessment which is derived from the Latin *assidere* meaning 'to sit with' (Earl, 2003). Learning and assessment therefore are not separate entities but complex intertwined processes. Indeed, assessment is learning (Earl, 2003) and should only exist to enable learning. If this is acknowledged in practice, the learner is assessed on the basis of performance rather than a test. Worawa Aboriginal College's commitment to holistic, personalised learning underpinned by formative, summative and self-assessment developed in the context of community provides a model which benefits all learners.

4 Discursive Curriculum

Taking the central issues of this discussion above into account, those of the interconnection between knowledge, culture and language, a school curriculum needs to be designed that will provide as many avenues as realistically possible into investigations of personal and community experience. In previous research that studied Gypsy/Roma/Traveller education in the United Kingdom and Indigenous identity and culture in Australian education, Hooley and Levinson (2014) proposed a set of principles and curriculum features for what they called 'Discursive Curriculum' (Table 5). In broad terms, discursive curriculum and learning can be described as involving language immersion (oral, written, community and formal), together with open, fluid and expansive arrangements that encourage student action, discussion, reflection and intellectual risk. It is intended that implementation of these principles will invoke an atmosphere and practice of respect, recognition and reciprocity, where students and teachers communicate, question and encourage each other as projects continue. It can be seen that the principles of country, community and language appear throughout with knowledge integrated and holistic in all domains of content and teaching. These principles and practices need to be implemented across the curriculum for all year levels to be successful.

Hopefully, the notion of 'discursiveness' will be supportive of Indigenous peoples in their struggle for cultural maintenance and survival. In regular

TABLE 5   Principles of discursive learning

Principle	Curriculum features
Learning requires respect for and recognition of different worldviews and learning	Philosophical investigation of knowledge, values, beliefs, viewpoints
Learning connects with the local and general physical and social environment	Country, geography, sacred sites, customs
Learning integrates local and general knowledge	Community and family events, oral and written history, stories, artefacts
Learning arises primarily from holistic knowledge, inquiry processes and language practices	Projects, themes, learning circles, celebrations, communication
Learning requires community interest, knowledge and experience	Community and family curriculum decision-making, history, events, stories, ideas, interpretations
Learning involves community members and Elders	Narratives and accounts, community visits, guest speakers, revered knowledge and wisdom
Learning occurs within community structures and protocols	Ways of knowing, community codes, ceremonies, conventions, extended time
Learning intensifies when 'community friends' assist knowledge production	Background and cross-cultural knowledge, advice, formal experience
Learning requires appropriate support structures	Community tutors, discussion sessions, meeting places, parent rooms, outreach scaffolding
Learning involves local and general protocols of monitoring, appraisal and consensus	Oral and written descriptions of learning in relation to local and general knowledge over extended time with community involvement

schooling, this will best be pursued through pragmatist notions of integrated knowledge and inquiry learning and negotiated projects that encourage small group learning. For example, projects that have as their capstone concern ecological and environmental aspects of the local area. After students have compiled a list of their interests and questions, they visit parents, Elders and community organisations to gather first-hand information about events such as droughts, bush fires and stories about rivers, lakes and animals. Reference can be made to newspaper articles, books and Internet to add background detail. When projects are completed, they can be displayed and discussed at community meetings for supplementary comment and suggestions for ongoing study. Combining history, science and humanities in this way enables the culture and language of all participants to be respected and to be integrated within a framework of understanding about local issues (Barnhardt & Kawagley, 2010). For those schools that follow a regular curriculum, it is realistic to propose that half the curriculum each week comprise integrated project work, while half the week is available for specific purpose workshops and studies. Over time, as projects are completed and validated by community consultation, a bank of material becomes available for study throughout the school. That is, projects undertaken by one group at a particular year level, can form the basis of investigation by other groups at other year levels and indeed, at other schools. This approach brings Indigenous and non-Indigenous students and families together with local knowledge, culture and language as the starting point and emphasises the social acts of personal and community investigation and experimentation, rather than the passive acceptance of educational authority and curriculum jurisdiction. Issues of student assessment are also considered in Chapter 7.

It is possible to track some progress that has been made in the broad directions noted above at a national policy level. For example, the body responsible for curriculum oversight in Australia has released Reconciliation Action Plan 2019–2022 that contains many important statements, such as the following (ACARA, 2019a, p. 7):

> The Aboriginal and Torres Strait Islander Histories and Cultures cross-curriculum priority provides the opportunity for Aboriginal and Torres Strait Islander peoples to access a culturally safe learning environment and the curriculum that recognises and celebrates their culture, history and identity. Furthermore, it provides young Australians who are not from an Aboriginal and Torres Strait Islander background the opportunity to gain a deeper understanding and appreciation of Aboriginal and Torres Strait Islander histories and cultures' deep knowledge, traditions and holistic worldviews.

National policy of this type draws attention to the place of history and culture in learning as well as the 'holistic world views' of Indigenous peoples. ACARA has worked with CSIRO, the national scientific and research body in Australia, to develop a set of resources for teachers called 'two way' science. A CSIRO scientist worked with a school and community to develop a two-way science learning program that 'included an investigation of the mamutjitji, or antlion, a type of insect. Elders taught students the Dreaming story that describes the structural features of the mamutjitji, and its special sand traps. This was connected to a scientific investigation of mamutjitji habitat.' The scientist, Mr Broun, commented that 'Two-way science is a pedagogy. It's an approach that connects the traditional ecological knowledge of Aboriginal people – that is the cultural understanding of people, animals and the environment – with western science inquiry and links that to the Australian Curriculum in a learning program' (ACARA, 2019b). This work authenticates Indigenous science as a field of investigation, problem-solving and community involvement that links closely with modern science in schools. There is no attempt here to claim that Indigenous science and modern science are the same, but there are substantial links across cultures, across ways of knowing and how ideas originate and are formulated.

5   Excursus 6: Meaning in Engines

I was at a loss. My car was difficult to start, the motor was sluggish and cutting out very quickly. My knowledge about flat batteries did not seem to be relevant. Fortunately, it was the school holidays, so there was a little bit of time to sort through my options. I decided to ring a good friend who knew about cars and had actually built one some years ago. He listened patiently to my story of disaster, asked a couple of questions, paused and then offered, 'Well, from what you have said, it could be a cracked head.' I had heard of that over the years, but had no idea what it meant. 'You could take out one of the spark plugs, turn on the engine, hold a piece of cardboard over the hole and see if any drops of water spits onto the card.' In due course, I managed to achieve this task and, that's exactly what happened, an amazing diagnosis. 'That seems to confirm it,' he announced placidly, 'what you need to do now is dismantle the engine and replace the gasket that has been cracked.' I'd heard a lot of silly ideas in my time, but this was the best: 'What do you mean, I've never done that before, I couldn't take an engine apart.' 'Of course you could, there's nothing to it,' was the reply, 'you just start at the top and take out each component in order.' There was little choice, if I wanted that car back in working order as soon as possible. I spread a bed sheet on the garage floor and proceeded to 'start at the top,' undoing nuts and bolts, laying them on the sheet, together with bits of metal, rubber hose and parts that I did not know existed. I was aware of the carburettor and the spark plugs, but that was about all. Ultimately, I had to remove what I now know to be the engine block, a very heavy piece of sold metal that just about ruined my back. But beneath, was the cause of the trouble, the thin head gasket separating the main halves of the block and yes, the crack was evident. With some exaltation, I manoeuvred the new gasket into place and began the reverse process of reassembly, nut by nut, piece by piece. Finally it was done and although starting fairly easily, the engine was running roughly, with coughs and spurts. 'Ah, that would be the timing,' said my friend with unruffled assurance, 'bring it over and I'll show you how to do the adjustments.' I now consider that I can speak with some authority around the barbeque on cracked heads and am willing to have a go at most mechanical repairs. And my advice to your response?: 'Of course you could, there's nothing to it.'

CHAPTER 7

Citizen Education

> It angers us when practices linked to the last century and the centuries before that, are still employed to deny the validity of Indigenous peoples' claim to existence, to land and territories, to the right of self-determination, to the survival of our languages and forms of cultural knowledge, to our natural resources and systems of living within our environments.
>
> LINDA TUHIWAI SMITH

∴

Formal and public education around the world should provide challenging and accessible learning and knowledge for all citizens regardless of socio-economic background. Indigenous culture and knowledge with its interests in anti-racist and equitable social relationships has a major contribution to make in identifying the dialectic of Indigenous and non-Indigenous knowing and the new progressive conceptions and practice that occur to improve schooling generally. This chapter proposes a form of citizen education that is located within a philosophy of practice, that recognises the dignity and knowledgeability of all peoples and which encourages the mutual flourishing of Indigenous and non-Indigenous experience alike.

1   Education as Philosophy of Practice

Considering formal education from a philosophical perspective of practice draws a clear line of distinction with conservative neoliberal viewpoints. Rather than imposing prespecified subject content from the dominant society, a practice-based understanding emerges from personal and community experience and culture that encourages 'living in' and 'living with' the social world. Not only does this involve attempting to establish 'meaning' of the world, but of 'listening' to what the world is saying. Conceived in this way, education is a process of becoming, of becoming more autonomous, more compassionate, more ethical. Living an ethical life is an 'action' structured by our humanness, guided by our political and cultural circumstances and proceeding socially with risk and uncertainty as we construct human being. Within this context, Indigenous and non-Indigenous peoples alike need to find their own level of existence and of learning and to manage the difficult competing factors of family, community and institution. Vygotsky and Chomsky saw language as a major aspect of humanness that enables connection between our inner and external modes, the active development of thought and speech in the formulation of ideas. Bakhurst (2007, p. 55) suggests that Vygotsky identified mind with consciousness through a 'system of higher mental functions' and explains:

> Mental phenomena take as their objects meaningful states of affairs in the world or representations thereof and any mental state can itself become the object of another: my thought can become the object of attention, reasoning, memory, volition and so forth. Any being capable of such reflexive mental acts is conscious. With this, consciousness is fundamentally related to meaning and Vygotsky concludes that 'consciousness as a whole has a semantic structure.' We might say that a conscious being occupies the space of meanings.

Consciousness remains one of the great unresolved questions of philosophy, but it provides a strategy for thinking about what it means to be human and therefore, how formal education should be arranged for everyone. In bringing together notions of language, consciousness and 'reflexive mental acts,' Vygotsky describes social being as an integrated existence within the social and physical environments with 'meaning' at its centre. This does not suggest that 'meaning' is given, to be found, correct and complete, but that we each come to our own understanding of what is real through continuing practice and discourse, through swimming in oceans of knowledge and experience. In the philosophical tradition of Dewey, Mead (Morris, 1934, p. 134) makes a significant comment when he draws these pragmatist threads together and is worth quoting in full:

> The evolutionary appearance of mind or intelligence takes place when the whole social process of experience and behaviour is brought within the experience of any one of the separate individuals implicated therein and when the individual's adjustment to the process is modified and refined by the awareness of consciousness which he thus has of it. It is by means of reflexiveness – the turning back of the experience of the individual upon himself – that the whole social process is thus brought into the experience of the individuals involved in it; it is by such means

which enable the individual to take the attitude of the other toward himself, that the individual is able consciously to adjust himself to that process and to modify the resultant of that process in any given social act in terms of his adjustment to it. Reflexiveness then, is the essential condition, within the social process, for the development of mind.

These are descriptive terms and how they play out for Indigenous and non-Indigenous peoples, that is for all humans, is still subject to conjecture. However, Mead's statement about 'reflexiveness' could not be more definite, but the notion of 'the turning back of experience' upon the awareness of the individual is difficult to grasp. It may be useful to think about this process in terms of sport. For example, a person playing golf and needing to chip the ball fifty metres to the green, quickly assesses the distance required, the direction of wind, the placement of the hole and stance taken towards the ball to obtain the most appropriate stroke. All of this planning occurs instantly and without apparent calculation or conscious thought. When the player judges which club to select and how strongly to hit the ball, what exactly has occurred in mind? What experience has been turned back on itself? The ball is observed as it arcs towards the green, lands and rolls towards the hole, in close proximity or further away. Instantly, the player evaluates and thinks what should be done next time. Mead describes this awareness as the adjustment made so that the person 'takes the attitude of the other' (in this case, the nature and behaviour of a golf ball in the natural environment) so that further acts are modified and understood more profoundly. This is a completely different organic process to the stimulus-response notion of conservative behaviourism involving a somewhat mechanical reaction to what impacts. Reflexivity also shows a willingness to observe and listen to the environment, a process of becoming part of the environment, so that the social acts of living and learning become as one. Humans then are 'self-organising' beings such that patterns and structures of thought are not imposed from the outside, but are constructed and established by the biological system itself. Chomsky refers to this process as human 'growth.'

Taking the above discussion into account envisages a different type of education for all children to that currently available in most countries. Education that respects the integrity of personal knowledge, culture and language will emphasise what it means to 'know' or exist in the world as 'subject,' defined by Biesta (2017, p. 57) as 'subject of our own actions, our own intentions and our own responsibilities,' not at the behest and superiority of others, but capable of our own sovereignty. This could be described as a 'world-centred,' or 'human-centred' understanding of education, where we take our place in the world and establish a life-long relationship with it and with others. Knowing is expressed as 'feeling' that we have intimate connection, a sense of satisfaction. While the concept of relationship is very important in its various forms, for the purposes of sovereign education, it means first and foremost a connectedness with country that pervades our very consciousness and every waking moment, such that social life is grounded in a naturalistic philosophy of being. It is not only land ownership or stewardship that is significant, but how humans understand their own existence in affinity and harmony. As has been mentioned previously, the intent of this line of thinking about education is not to impose a non-Indigenous or European concept of education on Indigenous or other groupings, but to share a more detailed framework of what it means to be human so that there is congruence between systems and structures and how families and children actually engage with their daily experience. While it is increasingly possible for Internet resources to provide what might be called technical answers to technical questions, there is a greater need than ever for shared and complex understandings of our humanness to enable diversity and history to be appreciated across cultures and economic backgrounds. Unfortunately and with the dominance of neoliberalism, it has proven to be extremely difficult for Indigeneity to be a sovereign construct of formal education, especially in relation to student capability. In this regard, we now turn to the apparently intractable concept of student assessment.

2 Assessment, the 'Hard Question' of Education

A major feature of the neoliberal world over the past fifteen years or so, has been the development of mass systems of testing at the national and international levels. In some respects, this has been a contradictory phenomenon, because neoliberal capitalism is not that interested in the educational achievement of individuals, but is primarily concerned with the performance of the market. Mass testing therefore is taken to be an economic indicator of how systems of education support production and profit for a country in relation to its competitors. In relation to our discussion above, current testing in schools is established on the completely wrong philosophical basis and does not reflect the predominant ways in which humans learn and formulate knowledge. It distracts from the authentic process of knowing and distorts the view that society has of its young people. As noted by Hooley (2015, pp. 75–76), there are two main points to bear in mind when considering whether the learning of children is deficient, or whether it is the ideology of traditional testing that cannot be accepted:

- Knowledge in formal educational programs is often considered from a logical positivist perspective. That is, the assumption of a linear progression from knowledge that can be known accurately by some and then be taught, learned, assessed and graded accurately for others. Knowledge is delivered, rather than built. Pragmatist and experiential knowledge on the other hand involves cycles of practice where knowledge of the world is built by each practitioner, discussed, monitored and evaluated by consensus and is provided with advice as a guide to and support for further learning.
- Assessment that assumes one approach to teaching and learning imposes a restrictive ideological and epistemological view of knowledge that accepts power and control by those who presume to know what is correct and have the right to impose their will on children and students generally. Under these circumstances, superficial learning in any class is restricted to a proportion of students and excludes those who prefer to learn in an interdisciplinary and inquiry manner drawing upon aesthetic, scientific and communicative experience.

It is difficult to ascertain exactly why the assessment of student learning at all levels remains the 'hard question' of education around the world. By this, it is meant that assessment does not really demonstrate the depth and intensity of what a person 'knows,' what is being considered by each subjectivity and consciousness, but in most cases provides a series of indicators that loosely connect what is in a student's mind with the context of the question being asked, that is, connections between internal and external states of being, a turning back of experience upon itself. Each person for example, needs to come to their own understanding of each object of experience, a thought, artefact, or physical item such as wheel, giraffe, sadness, or how to act, within the context of the views of others, but ultimately as they conceptualise the world. Of course, education systems can ignore these philosophical ideas and test as they see fit, the common practice worldwide. Essays can be written, questions can be answered, problems can be posed, physical exercises can be attempted, paintings and music can be composed. What these tasks actually tell us about human understanding of their social experience is another matter. Perhaps neoliberal education systems are not interested in what students 'feel' they 'know' and merely sift and sort cohorts until a few remain to participate with the command sectors of the economy. There are however much higher community expectations for the education system than that.

At this point, a set of principles regarding the monitoring of student learning is proposed below, based on a pragmatist philosophical view of human knowledge:

- That formal schooling locates the child at the centre of the educative process and therefore constructs curriculum around the interests of the child rather than the political and economic imperatives of the nation state.
- That formal schooling is framed by an explicit philosophy of knowledge such that the child is enabled to explore personal social and physical environments from a democratic and integrated, inquiry-based perspective.
- That formal schooling emphasises negotiated project-based learning in association with specific knowledge workshops such as arts, humanities, sciences and technologies connected with language and mathematical understandings and practices.
- That formal schooling monitor student learning through school-based portfolios of learning artefacts within agreed criteria and compiled over extensive periods of time.
- That formal schooling adopts assessment procedures that assure assessment informs learning.
- That formal schooling monitor systemic features through compilation of samples of school-based portfolios within agreed criteria and collected every two years across Years 4–6 and across Years 8–10.
- That formal schooling emphasises the artefacts of language immersive, integrated knowledge and descriptive inquiry learning for monitoring of student learning, rather than the accumulation of predetermined information at specific age levels.
- That formal schooling through processes of school-based portfolios of learning artefacts ensure that socio-cultural and language background is respected and that collective as well as individual experience is recognised.
- That formal schooling includes moderation of school-based portfolios of learning artefacts across groups of local schools or within larger regions.

Principles such as the above reorient schooling to professional governance and processes that authorise knowledge arising from personal experience, discourse, reflection and judgement, for Indigenous and non-Indigenous children (Lowe et al., 2019). This does not preclude suggested contexts of learning, or the inclusion of a range of assessment procedures for particular purpose. These are decisions to be made by the profession at the systemic and school levels.

There seems little basis to assume that certain sections of the population are not capable of engaging with all aspects of knowledge. This has been an issue with public education since the end of World War II and the development and expansion of secondary education in many countries. It has been extremely difficult if not impossible to design and implement formats of schooling that do not contribute to social division and stratification present in the broader society. For example, the famous Education Act of 1944 in England established a system of comprehensive schools that had open entry for all students, as distinct from selective entry schools based on academic background and test results. Comprehensive schooling enabled greater access for working class children including girls, but its actual nature and curriculum remain somewhat contested to this day. In his famous ethnographic book, Willis (1978), described the experience of a group of working class boys in England, how they saw and responded to school life and why it was that 'working class kids get working class jobs.' It may be that little has changed in England and similar countries today (Reay, 2017). In Australia, the Karmel (1973) Report formally established the concept of educational 'disadvantage' and identified priority issues such as inequalities of provision and opportunity, general lack of funding including from both state and federal governments and a need to improve the quality of teaching and curriculum. As a means of coping with educational disadvantage, the Disadvantaged Schools Program was created and continued for over twenty years, providing funding to schools on a submission basis. Over time, a considerable amount of this funding was allocated to the employment of teacher aides in support of specific programs in schools. The Karmel Report recognised that it was not possible for schools to 'compensate' for social inequality, but that increased resources could provide a more enriching and engaging curriculum for all students regardless of background. The question of 'disadvantage' is a vexed one, implying that some students are disadvantaged intellectually in comparison to others, perhaps because of some evolutionary mistake in DNA. As mentioned previously, this view has been strengthened over recent years through highly doubtful statistical correlations that are made via mass testing and for example, connecting test results with family income. Standardised mass testing is designed to 'measure' predetermined bands of information that can be disconnected from the learner's personal culture, language and experience and thereby give a completely false notion of 'disadvantage.' Many Indigenous, working class people and those on very low income, do find daily and family survival a difficult task, but to confuse (deliberately or otherwise) social inequality, racism and division with intellectual deficit, is a horrendous, unforgiveable mistake.

It is clear that consideration is being given to changing the nature of mass testing regimes, as society and industry changes. From his position as Director for Education and Skills, OECD, Schliecher (2018) comments on technological influences on schooling that will inevitably lead to different approaches to teaching and testing:

> When we could still assume that what we learn in school will last for a lifetime, teaching content knowledge and routine cognitive skills was rightly at the centre of education. Today, the world no longer rewards us just for what we know – Google knows everything – but for what we can do with what we know. The more knowledge that technology allows us to search and access, the more important becomes deep understanding and the capacity to make sense out of content.

This debate is incomplete, but it seems that there is a shift away from a focus on traditional knowledge, to other sociological and indeed psychological concepts such as emotional stability, well-being, resilience and the like. Whether or not the outcome will be 'deep understanding' and the 'capacity to make sense of content' and whether or not testing procedures can in fact 'measure' these characteristics remains to be seen. For Indigenous communities and for those whose culture and way of life are also in contradiction to dominant schooling systems, more rather than fewer challenges await. Resolving the 'hard question' of knowledge and assessment of student learning will require a much more rigorous understanding of education as philosophy of practice than currently exists.

In considering the contradictions that exist between the natural world and cultural practices that have been established by nations, institutions and communities, Dewey (1989, p. 41) wrote about rapid social change in a positive and negative sense in the years leading up to World War II, 'but without corresponding readjustment of the basic emotional and moral attitudes formed in the period prior to change of environment.' Dewey's thinking at the time was prompted by events such as the Great Depression, the rise of totalitarianism and the spectre of war, but are equally relevant today. He placed importance not only on the habits and customs formed by interaction with the natural environment, but the relationship of these with the features of experience and culture that surround us every hour of the day. Racism, discrimination and war as well as the development of shared values, kindness and harmony arise from this dialectical and dynamic relationship, emphasising the need for understanding and balance by all concerned. Dewey went on to comment:

> No estimate of the effects of culture upon the elements that now make up freedom begins to be adequate that does not take into account the moral and religious splits that are found in our very make up as persons. The problem of creation of genuine democracy cannot be successfully dealt with in theory or in practice save as we create intellectual and moral integration out of present disordered conditions.

3 Citizen Knowledge, Truth and Freedom

Throughout the previous brief chapters, a portrait of what it means to be human has been sketched, a philosophical portrait that applies to all humans regardless of their socio-economic and cultural backgrounds. There are differences depending on geography and landscape, on community histories and struggles, on the particulars of language and experience. But overall there is a great unity of the peoples of the world, in the notion of personal independence and how we engage realities and make sense of what is observed and contemplated. While conservative behaviourism has provided one possible outline, it is the practice-based and cultural understandings of Vygotsky, Chomsky and the pragmatists amongst others who have provided the colour, detail and format for the inherent qualities and expression of humanness. Chomsky's view of language as another system of human biology that occurs through growth, in the same way as systems of vision, breathing and circulation of the blood occurs, shows a concept of what it means to be human for all people and lays the basis of respect for all sovereign individuals and groups. Indigenous and non-Indigenous communities share this common heritage and this common future.

From the above discussion, there are close connections that can be drawn between the educational program at Worawa and main points discussed in Chapters 1, 3, 4, 5 and 6 of this book (Table 6). As has been noted previously, these major points have an epistemological perspective, or a philosophical understanding of human knowledge as the basis of interacting with the social and physical environment for engagement and meaning. From a pragmatist point of view, each of us has to come to our own understanding of each object of thought. We have to define and know for ourselves objects such as wheel, leaf, rain, frog. Experience and thought must therefore be as one. Emphasising social practice and the theorising of such practice as being at the centre of human consciousness is not a new idea, but the integration of practice and theorising across all aspects of the school curriculum to respect this outlook is not handled well by many education systems around the world. Worawa Aboriginal College therefore has much to offer the world, philosophically and educationally.

Many other features of social life need to be explained from within a pragmatist philosophical position. Features such as values, freedom, truth and ethics. These can be laid down by experts and the powerful, or be constructed by participants and the ordinary. Values for instance arise from human experience over the centuries when it is generally agreed that certain actions are more appropriate than others under specific circumstances. Ethical conduct has the

TABLE 6 Summary of key issues from Chapters 1, 3, 4, 5 and 6

Issue	Description
Education	That human education is conceived as philosophy of practice for engagement and meaning
Context	That formal education takes place within dominant economic, political and traditional features of society, increasingly global neoliberalism
Practice	That human practice centres on integration of doing and thinking for desired and mutual purpose
Pragmatism	That conception of all the effects of an object (thought, idea, artefact) makes the whole of our understanding of the object, enabling processes of integrated knowledge and inquiry learning
Knowledge	That human knowledge arises from interaction with social and physical environment for meaning and purpose
Culture	That culture is considered as way of life of a particular group of people involving customs, ceremony, country, community
Language	That language is identified as human act, to establish next act

same genesis. Freedom can be thought of as the capability of groups of people to reach consensus on what it means to experience mind, to act, think, know and create, ethically. 'To experience mind' is taken to mean human awareness of personal consciousness, thought and language such that ongoing cycles of social acts, thinking and reflection can occur to pursue human interest. Freedom is conceived as arising collectively rather than individually and can be pursued to a greater or lesser extent within any country regardless of the prevailing economic system. Under these constraints however, freedom is mediated by layers of economic, political and cultural factors. John Stuart Mill's famous treatise 'On Liberty' (Mill, 1839/1998) in which he advocated that men and women should be able to act freely without interference from society or the state and provided no harm came to others, was a significant understanding of freedom, although its emphasis on individual rights is difficult to establish in the complexities of the nation state and globalised economies of today. Two versions of truth are also possible to conceive within a practice and pragmatist framework. In the first instance, there are local truths generally substantiated by community experience over time, such as when the first occurrence of snow will occur every winter, or whether neighbours from across the plains can be trusted. Then there are more general truths such as the appearance of the moon in the night sky year-by-year, or that most people from all villages are kind and generous given the opportunity. In this way, human practice, or what can be envisaged as cultural practice, enables our understanding of the world through our experience of it, to be observed, described, contested and theorised until an equilibrium of viewpoints is obtained. The endpoint of this process is unknown, except it can generate both the good and the bad along the way, each of which needs to be worked through for the mutual benefit of all. From social acts to ethical conduct constitutes the reality of human existence.

A model of what can be called 'Citizen Education' is now proposed, bringing together key social and educational ideas from history and around the world discussed in chapters above and applying to all people recognised under the law as being a legal or customary member of the state or nation. Citizenship of the dominant society as a concept may not be accepted by all groups existing within the nation state, but it is used here as a general mark of respect for all those who wish to be recognised as a member of society or grouping with full rights and obligations. Isin (2009, p. 368) nominates the need for 'a new vocabulary of citizenship' in changing times such that:

> What seems now obvious is that throughout the twentieth century (and accelerating towards its end) rights, sites, scales and acts of citizenship have proliferated to the extent that these have begun to change our dominant figure of citizenship. We have yet to accept this fully let alone understand it. I will call this figure 'activist citizenship' and its actors 'activist citizens' to contrast it sharply with the figure of 'active citizenship' that emerged during the French Revolution and that persisted for two centuries.

The notion of 'active citizenship' arising from the French Revolution conferred voting rights for the Legislative Assembly on males who paid taxes of a certain amount. Universal suffrage around the world where all citizens are considered equal is still an aspiration for many as the elimination of Apartheid in South Africa attests. Similarly, having a respected 'voice' that is 'heard' by decision makers, remains an ongoing struggle for many Indigenous peoples (see Uluru Statement from the Heart, Chapter 1). On the basis of 'activist citizenship' and 'activist citizens' within the neoliberal state therefore, a conception of formal 'Citizen Education' can be envisaged as constituted by four interrelated practices framing the organisation of schooling generally and of particular studies for all students regardless of background (Figure 4). Under this arrangement and initially, all teacher and student participants in a secondary school humanities project for example are considered as living and learning within

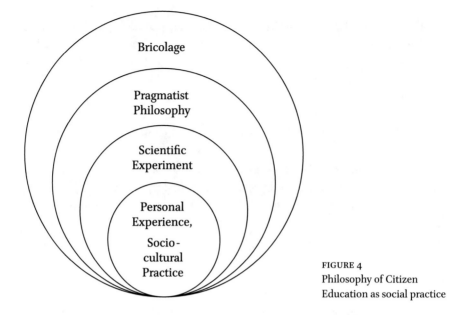

FIGURE 4
Philosophy of Citizen Education as social practice

the French social construct of 'bricolage,' whereby new works or outcomes are created by the use of materials and processes at hand. These are flexible, creative and open-ended processes as the need arises.

Drawing on the understandings of Levi-Strauss (1968) and Denzin and Lincoln (2000/2017), Kincheloe (2005) argued for the concept of teacher and student as 'bricoleur' so that diverse ideas, strategies and materials are accepted and brought together in the process of inquiry, teaching and research. In this way, all school topics must begin with and document the interests of participants so that a broad practice framework of knowledge, language and culture is established as the underpinning of the topic. They cannot be made invisible, denied or ignored. Accordingly, working within the bricolage as bricoleur will alter the relationships between participants and recognise the talents that each brings to the tasks at hand (Shay, 2020). This means that a pragmatist philosophy of knowledge guides the investigation, with knowing and doing being socially situated and respected for the social realities that have generated specific understandings of participants. Within the pragmatist environment, scientific experiments are negotiated, designed and conducted to explore certain aspects of the (sciences or humanities) topic such as diary entries, interviews, role plays, video extracts, Internet materials and the like. At the heart of this overall process, is the grounding that participants have from their personal and community experience and as noted above, from the values, truths and ethical conduct that guide their relationships with knowledge and with co-investigators. There may be tensions that exist along the way, as different socio-cultural practices and interests of teachers and students need to be accommodated, but this is an essential aspect of the philosophy of practice. This proposed model of 'Citizen Education' certainly accords with the criterion of 'activist citizenship' and 'activist citizen' as suggested by Isin and ensures that the rights and obligations of all students and teachers must be included as an educational if not human right. The model provides for groups of Indigenous students to work together on specific projects as appropriate, perhaps as agreed with local Elders, or for learning circles of Indigenous and non-Indigenous students to collaborate on integrated projects that interface across cultural groupings. Knowledge exemplars as described in Chapter 2 will be regular outcomes, with ungraded descriptions of student progress, exhibited, discussed and validated at community meetings. As respected and active participatory residents within their own school fraternity and family communities, students from diverse socio-economic backgrounds can take their rightful place as cultured and knowledgeable citizens creating a more just and compassionate society for all. At some point, discrimination, racism and exclusion will become historical oddities.

4   Excursus 7: International Friendship

It was a mild and sunny day as a small group of community members, students and lecturers made their way through the forest of eucalypt trees and red gums to the banks of the Murray River in south eastern Australia. We had discussed the origins of the river before, the local Indigenous story of how the large Murray cod in searching through the mud and rocks had provided tunnels, channels and billabongs for the water to flow, compared with early maps and geological features that showed how the river had changed course through flood and shifting land. Both explanations sat easily side-by-side for local culture and existence. We were on our way to meet a group of visiting native Canadians from the Kehewin Performance and Resource Network, who had expressed the wish to pay their respects to the Indigenous community. In due course, we stood in a circle near the water's edge, four native Canadians, four Elders from the nearby town and six or seven students from our teacher education university program. I realised the honour that had been accorded me in being invited to attend as a non-Indigenous lecturer from the big and remote city but still relatively unknown to the community. Over the next hour or so, stories were shared such as the importance of the river in providing food and how local people would swim out and then dive down to grab ducks and fowl for dinner that night. I remember our native Canadian friends talking about how the circle in many native societies includes the understanding that all creatures and elements of nature are bound by a family tie. All creatures are respected in song, dance and oral histories, while the directions of north, south, east and west have different meanings for each nation within the circle. Many dances and ceremonies follow the path of the sun. Towards the end of our discussion, one of the native Canadians produced a booklet that their group had prepared entitled 'Inside the Circle.' The chapters of the booklet were constructed in such a way to ensure recognition of the circle of seasons and to respect environmental awareness. For example, spring is seen as a time of rebirth, ceremony and celebration and a time for social gatherings and reflection on environmental issues of greatest concern for each particular nation. Each section began with an oral history and was written as a base for story tellers to use. Interestingly, it was accepted that the stories could be embellished so that they could become personal and connected to local experience. I was overcome and deeply honoured when our visitors unexpectedly presented the booklet to me as an expression of friendship between the Indigenous and non-Indigenous peoples of Australia and Canada. As I stood there, many years ago, on the banks of the Murray River, surrounded by the quietness of the bush, but also the shared culture, knowledge and wisdom of humble, ordinary people, I understood the place of collective experience in living with the world and grappling with its complexities, difficulties and beauty. I realised our mutual existence 'inside the circle.'

CHAPTER 8

The Invincible Spirit, Defining the Future

The River is Us – Carrying the Spirit and Strength of Dungala
LOIS PEELER

∴

Proud Yorta Yorta woman, activist and educator Dr Lois Peeler explored how respect for Indigenous knowledge could and should change modern Australia at the annual Dungala Kaiela Oration on Wednesday 9 September 2020. Dr Peeler is Executive Director/Principal of Australia's only Aboriginal girls' boarding school, Worawa Aboriginal College and has held senior positions in the community and public sectors. Her oration reprinted below, 'The River is Us – Carrying the Spirit and Strength of Dungala,' explores how Aboriginal knowledge, narrative and shared stories have mainstream importance for survival, emotional health and the general wellbeing of all humanity.

⋯

Let me begin by honouring our spirit ancestor of Yorta Yorta country, Baiaimi. I also honour our past leaders who have paved the way for us today. I pay my respects to Elders past and present and emerging. My apical ancestors were river people, my mother's mother was Yarmuk of the Dhulanyagan Clan of Ulupna. My father was Woiwurrung on his father's side and Yorta Yorta on his mother's side. His mother's mother was from the Moira Clan of the great Moria Forest on the banks of Dhungala. I identify as Yorta Yorta through my mother and Woiwurrung/Wurundjeri through my father whose ancestral river was Birrarung, the Yarra. I grew up in my mother's country. Yorta Yorta people are river people, our beliefs, traditions, sustenance, existence and stories come from our ancestral river, Dungala.

Nancy Cato in her book, *Mister Maloga*, which chronicles the history of Maloga Aboriginal Mission under Danial Matthews, wrote about the clans which gathered in the sandhills of the Great Bend were all river people. They came from an area of forty mile radius around Echuca, *The Meeting of the Waters*. They came from the winding Wakool to the north or from the Yacoa to the south, from

Kyabram, the *Great Forest*, or Nathalia, the *Place with No Stones*. Some paddled all the way down the Kiama or Goulburn River. The rivers the clans came from included the Murray, the Goulburn, the Broken, Campaspe, the Edwards. They called the big river, Tongala, the Great Water.

The Murray river is sacred to Yorta Yorta Dreaming, in this context in the Aboriginal world view, the Goulburn and Broken rivers that feed the Murray are of immense importance. As river people, other rivers that flow into the Murray such as the Campaspe and Edwards rivers are identified as being of importance, but of lesser importance. The senior Elders stated that 'It all flows into the Murray anyway, so it is all the same.' My grandmother, Yarmuk often spoke of her earliest memories of the Murray, which she wrote about in *From Old Maloga: The memoirs of an Aboriginal Woman*, published in 1947. She wrote: 'I remember when I was three, Mr Matthews came, my brother and sister and I ran and hid near the bank of the river. White man coming to take us away,' she said. 'We were terrified, we were in a big dray with four horses and Mr Matthews was collecting all Aborigines along the river. Mr Matthews took us to the Maloga Mission.'

> The real value is in accepting that the common experience of all humanity is vital for the whole people to survive and thrive.

As a proud custodian of generations of knowledge, I can work towards recording and disseminating information. However it is not only information that is required. I pose the question, is our story respected and valued? Knowledge acquisition is important, but a singular focus is somewhat misplaced. The imperative is also on hearing. I am not able to effect change on that platform. Today I share with you in the hope that the hearing matches the cost of the sharing. Respect is so much more than creating a quiet space for the words and lives of others. Respect comes from a deep corporate and individual understanding that others value. Therefore respect and value are integrated to such an extent as to be homogenous, one is dependent on the other. Without valuing, there is no respect. The importance of the Collected River Stories and Histories is not in the acquiesced domain of sharing knowledge, or in the safe keeping of facts and narrative, although that is vital. The real value is in accepting that the common experience of all humanity is vital for the whole people to survive and thrive. Learning that all stories have innate power and all stories make for life strengthening and connecting, is the beginning of a healthy, national metanarrative. Until Aboriginal narrative, understandings, knowledge and spirituality are more than curios, or benevolent additions to Eurocentric compilations, then there will be no real valuing them to Aboriginal participants, beyond a salve to colonial cringe and the satisfaction of justice appearing to be done.

Our stories must be transmitted, adopted and held as sacred by all if they are to empower our shared futures. The value of our oral history is in the identification of the resilience of our people and also in the potential of those stories to add to their own richness and depth to the greater Australian narrative. With the details and facts communicated through the voices and memories of Elders, comes new ways to move ahead as we understand the complexities of our intersections, parallels and collisions. Aboriginal knowledge and narrative has mainstream importance for survival, emotional health and the general well-being of all humanity. We have a rightful place in the academic, philosophical and political arenas, that far surpass the value of preserving Indigenous cultures and ancient ways. Yes, preservation is important, but more important is recognition and interaction with the knowledge that is shared. The gap in uptake of health, law, relational knowledge and education is still cavernous.

Mainstream Australia has not availed itself of the library of information on seasons, preservation of flora and fauna, caring for country on land and waters that the world's longest living culture embodies. Only true value and respect will enable this knowledge to be received and utilised in the modern Australian context. Without our stories, our understandings, we will all be poorer, poorer in every way. When this knowledge and understanding is integrated into the Australian psyche, then we will begin to truly grow, diversify and enrich what it is to be a nation of people who have innate respect for original peoples as First Nations peoples. I believe we have a way to go. When such a grand integration occurs, there will be a national identity that rivals any other, while the many cultures that make up Australia will remain distinct, a new identity where there is national pride in Aboriginal culture will emerge. Australia then will have a culture as unique and resilient as the animals that live on the land.

So in this oration, I offer knowledge and a proud tradition of rising up to engage, inform and bring change to a culture that was foreign and hostile toward us, the peoples of Dungala. As for shared vision, well that will emanate from shared sight, sight that is focused on a future where there is equality so deeply ingrained that we look ahead with such congruence so that the vision is richer, greater and brighter for all. The new vision will only be clear when the lens is equally Indigenous and non-Indigenous. This is a continuation of my desire and commitment to pay tribute to those who have gone before, to reflect on the challenges and honour the achievements of our change makers.

In 2008, I undertook an Aboriginal oral history project and authored the report as part of the City of Greater Shepparton *River Connect* program. *The Cultural Landscape of The Flat* chronicled the experiences of Aboriginal people who set off from *The Flat* which followed the historic 1939 *Walk Off* from Cummeragunja. First dispossessed of traditional lands – gathered together on 'reserved land' – under authoritarian regime, our men had petitioned the government for a portion of land to farm. They cleared the land and made agrarian success of the small farmland. To have it confiscated was a second assault when the land was taken back and leased to graziers. The poor management and authoritarian regime of the Cummeragunja Aboriginal Station, combined with the threat of removal of children, galvanised the residents of Cummeragunja to leave the reserve. The *Walk Off* came as a final desperate response to have basic freedoms and the ability to thrive taken from our people. The story of one Elder provides stark insight into life on Cummeragunja.

The laws and restrictions on Cummeragunja Station were very tough for our people. A lot of decisions were left to the manager of the reserve and if he didn't like a person, he could give them a hard time. I know some of our people who used to speak up for their rights were expelled. Living there, you were always under threat, if you did something wrong in the manager's eyes, you were confronted with either being expelled or the police would pick you up. The manager threatened to cut off people's rations if they didn't conform to his ways of running the reserve. And in remembering the *Walk Off* he said, 'I remember quite plainly that day, I was sixteen years of age when our people packed their belongings in the old buggy, some walked, some sailed their canoes across the river, others crossed the river Murray into Victoria on the punt with their belongings.

> Change is possible when there is a shared investment in the recording and sharing of lived experience of previously unheard and unheeded people.

The collection of oral histories was undertaken in a spirit of generosity and a desire by the participants for the wider community to hear and understand an Aboriginal perspective about their lived experience, a sincere desire to share the depth and breadth and impact of this experience gave the impetus for the creation of the body of information and experience. And, as I expressed earlier, the project was an attempt to circumvent mere knowing and penetrate to deep hearing and understanding. History was being recorded, the voices belonged to those who lived this history, those people who in their youth were not listened to or even given the right to speak for themselves had a platform to share. They came to speak and free themselves from some of the burdens of the past, but more than anything, to ensure the stories are recorded and remembered, to ensure there is the potential for their own history to last and to be cherished.

The greatest hope is that in the saving and the telling of these facts, images and stories that there will be an opportunity for change. Change is possible when there is a shared investment in the recording and sharing of lived experience of previously unheard and unheeded people. These spoken accounts of personal experience, feelings, memories and opinions are of people who participated in historically significant events in which they were deeply involved, whose feelings and memories are far from detached and which are accordingly incredibly valuable, valuable beyond the narrative, valuable as a catalyst for change. These stories must not just be enjoyed, studied or recorded, for them to have power they must be embraced as part of this human experience, the Australian experience, valued, integrated, learnt from, heard, embedded.

The Oral History Collection program gives voice to the Aboriginal people's stories, remembrances and experiences. Now some of the memories and experiences of that period may not be particularly palatable within the context of the contemporary cultural vibrancy of the City of Greater Shepparton. However during the period in which the stories were told, Aboriginal people were not treated as full citizens of Australia and faced many legal disadvantages and discriminations. Let me say too, that philosophy and attitudes behind these policies were ingrained in the hearts and minds of many of the regions residents. Like any genetic code or nurtured trait, these beliefs do not merely dissipate with time, often they must be exposed, excised and exercised. Embracing these stories and historical experience, then adding them to national curriculum and records will not be enough to effect change to the Australian psyche. There must be some defined action to rebuild, renew and absorb. Our national DNA needs to be altered and this is no small thing. The collection of Elder's oral histories was undertaken in a spirit of generosity and a desire by participants for the wider community to hear and understand an Aboriginal perspective about their experience.

As it is for any people who have survived and thrived under considerably difficult circumstances, there is an intermingling of pride and suffering in the retelling. Of course, there is some bitterness, but the overriding motivation is the desire to create something better for all. The achievements of Yorta Yorta people are a testament to the resilience and strength of our old people who sought to create a better life for future generations. Our people have produced accountants, academics, doctors, nurses, magistrates, teachers, poets, principals, teachers and elite sports people, spiritual leaders, senior public servants, community leaders, musicians, theatre writers and actors, artists and singers. In fact, the Cummeragunja choir was the starting point for singers of oral genres, gospel, country, fold, soul, pop, blues, opera and even Eurovision participants.

Let us be clear. The struggle continues.

Our past leaders were at the forefront of calls for equality and self-determination. Consider that the historic Day of Mourning held on 26 January 1939 organised by Aboriginal leaders of the day, but motivated by lived experience of life on an Aboriginal reserve and key leaders in the organisation and conduct of the event, included our Yorta Yorta people, Jack Pattern, William Cooper, Doug Nichols and Aunty Marj Tucker, these are our heroes. Their names are etched into the history books of Indigenous Australia. They are added to the eons of our stories and reflect our true beliefs and traditions. They embody our spirit. It is my belief that if Australia is to be whole and vital, these Aboriginal heroes must become national heroes, who we celebrate with pride and ownership, not as separate heroes of Aboriginal history, but rather as individuals of national significance and pride. This will be achieved when our children learn about them at school and study them at university. It will be achieved when Aboriginal stories become celebrated and embraced as life blood of what it means to be Australian. Let us be clear, that the struggle continues.

Aboriginal community leaders of today are involved in efforts at decolonising government and tertiary institutions and to manage our own affairs, to drive down the rate of our children coming into contact with the justice system and the appalling incarceration rate of our people. The *Royal Commission into Aboriginal Deaths in Custody* (Australian Government, 1991) found that the high rates of Aboriginal deaths in custody was directly related to underlying factors of poor health and housing, unemployment and education levels, dysfunctional families and communities, dispossession and past government policies. It concluded that the most significant contributing factor leading Aboriginal people into conflict with the justice system was their disadvantage and unequal position in relation to the wider society. Our people have long-called for self-determination and in recent times, the notion of self-determination has gained traction with governments. I believe however that many are grappling with the true meaning of self-determination. As a people who experience control of every facet of our lives, we avidly pursue self-determination.

We know what's best for our community. Consider the achievements led by our community in the establishment of Aboriginal organisations such as health services, the legal service, housing service, child care and many more, including Victoria's only Aboriginal school, Worawa Aboriginal College. Aboriginal people have always made valuable contributions to the economic, sporting and social development of the region and still do. Our organisations are the life blood of the community and major employers of Aboriginal people across the region. In the Shepparton district alone, Aboriginal initiatives include First Nations Credit Union, Rumbalara Aboriginal Community Medical Centre, Rumbalara Football Netball Club, Rumbalara Aged Care, child care,

Kaiela Arts, Munarra Regional Centre for Excellence, Dungala Kaiela Oration. We have a vision, a place-based approach, to create a holistic future for our people, our children, our youth, our Elders.

> Our stories are meaningful, as we share our stories we are sharing the past and our present and our beliefs, we are sharing the river, the spirit of the land and the lives on it. It is all one story.

The stories of our people in our oral history collection demonstrates our resilience, our strength and determination. In terms of community development, we have the capacity, we have the determination and the commitment. In this context, it is pleasing that the refreshed *Closing the Gap* (Australian Government, 2020) framework, is moving towards an agenda that partners with Aboriginal and Torres Strait Islander people, enables more community control and embeds shared decision making. This approach is based on local action, a determination to make a difference and to achieve change.

As I said earlier, we do have a vision, actually, a planned project. This substantial work has been done by the Kaiela Institute which has defined the following overarching objectives that this project should support: To develop a rights-based platform that recognises Yorta Yorta people's rights to an economy and a future state of productivity post-dispossession; to set a clear regional trajectory towards Indigenous parity and prosperity; to activate the Aboriginal economy in our region through direct investment and support for enterprise development and entrepreneurship; reposition the perceived social, cultural and economic value of the contribution of Aboriginal people, heritage and enterprise to our region; to build regional accountability for improving Aboriginal social, economic and cultural position by defining activity and outcomes in a way that is specific and measurable. Central to it success is a co-ordinated approach and shared vision in improving the socio-economic position of the whole community. With an Aboriginal population of around 3500 in the Shepparton region, the vision is for better health, education and economic outcomes that help counter current disadvantage, including intergenerational disadvantage.

Increasingly Aboriginal communities across the country are seeking to enter into partnerships to improve the position of our people in a holistic sense, that is the physical, social, emotional, spiritual, cultural and economic well-being, bringing about total well-being for our communities. Underpinning all is the invincible spirit of our people and the spiritual, social and personal relationship in connection with our ancestral river and environs. My sister, Hyllus Maris, a remarkable woman who was an activist, poet, playwright and most importantly, my sister. She expressed this in the poem that she wrote, *Spiritual Song of the Aborigine* – let me quote a few lines from that poem:

> I am a child of the Dreamtime people
> part of this land like the gnarled gum tree
> I am the river softly singing
> chanting our songs on the way to the sea.

Our stories are meaningful, as we share our stories we are sharing the past and our present and our beliefs, we are sharing the river, the spirit of the land and the lives on it. It is all one story. My hope today is that each of you will be able to hear the stories, sense the importance of the river, understand the connectedness and become one with them.

Thank you and good night.

References

ACARA. (2019). *The Australian curriculum*. Australian Curriculum, Assessment and Reporting Authority (ACARA). https://www.acara.edu.au/

ACARA. (2019a). *ACARA reconciliation action plan July 2019–July 2022*. Australian Curriculum, Assessment and Reporting Authority (ACARA). https://www.acara.edu.au/docs/default-source/corporate-publications/updated-rap-2019.pdf/

ACARA. (2019b). *Teaching two-way science in Aboriginal and Torres Strait Islander communities*. Australian Curriculum, Assessment and Reporting Authority (ACARA). https://www.acara.edu.au/docs/default-source/Media-Releases/20190318-two-way-science-media-release.pdf?sfvrsn=2/

Ahmed, W. (2018). *The polymath: Unlocking the power of human versatility*. Wiley.

Ailey. (n.d.). *Alvin Ailey American Dance Theatre*. Retrieved November 16, 2020, from https://www.alvinailey.org/

Allen, R. (2012). Supporting struggling students with academic rigor. *Educational Leadership*, 54(8), 3–5.

Andrews, M. (2019). *Journey into dreamtime*. Ultimate World Publishing.

ANKN. (2020). *Alaska native knowledge network*. The University of Alaska Fairbanks. https://www.uaf.edu/ankn/

Alangui, W. (2003). Searching for mathematical ideas in stone walls. In *Proceedings of the 26th annual conference of the Mathematics Education Research Group of Australasia*, 1 (pp. 57–64).

Apple, M. W. (2006). Understanding and interrupting neoliberalism and neoconservatism in education. *Pedagogies: An International Journal*, 1(1), 21–26.

Archibald, J.-A., Lee-Morgan, J. B. J., & De Santolo, J. (2019). *Decolonising research: Indigenous storywork as methodology*. Zed Books Ltd.

Australian Government. (1991). *Royal commission into Aboriginal deaths in custody*. National Archives of Australia. Retrieved November 16, 2020, from https://www.naa.gov.au/explore-collection/first-australians/royal-commission-aboriginal-deaths-custody/

Australian Government. (2020). *Closing the gap: In partnership*. Retrieved November 16, 2020, from https://ctgreport.niaa.gov.au/

Bakhurst, D. (2007). Vygotsky Demons. In H. Daniels, M. Cole, & J. V. Wertsch (Eds.), *The Cambridge companion to Vygotsky* (pp. 50–76). Cambridge University Press. https://doi.org/10.1017/CCOL0521831040.003

Ball, S. (2012). *Global Education Inc: New policy networks and the neoliberal imaginary*. Taylor & Francis Ltd. https://doi.org/10.4324/9780203803301

Bangara. (n.d.). *Bangarra Dance Theatre*. Retrieved November 20, 2020, from https://www.bangarra.com.au/

Barnhardt, R., & Kawagley, A. O. (Eds.). (2010). *Alaska native education: Views from within*. Alaska Native Knowledge Network.

Battiste, M. (2015). *Decolonising education: Nourishing the learning spirit*. Purich Publishing Limited.

Beatty, R. (2016, August 15). *Exploring Indigenous culturally responsive mathematics*. The Learning Exchange: Engage, Innovatec Change. https://thelearningexchange.ca/culturally-responsive-mathematics/

Begg, A. (2000, August 22). *Enactivism: A personal interpretation*. Paper presented at Stirling University. Retrieved November 20, 2020, from http://www.ioe.stir.ac.uk/docs/Begg%20Enactivism%20.DOC

Biesta, G. (2017). *Letting art teach*. ArtEZ Press.

Biesta, G. (2018). What if? Art education beyond expression and creativity. In C. Naughton, G. Biesta, & D. R. Cole (Eds.), *Art, artists and pedagogy: Philosophy and the arts in education* (Chapter 2). Routledge. https://doi.org/10.4324/9781315143880

Bronfenbrenner, U. (1979). *The ecology of human development: Experiments by nature and design*. Harvard University Press.

Cajete, G. A. (2019). Envisioning Indigenous education: Applying insights from Indigenous views of teaching and learning. In E. McKinley & L. Smith (Eds.), *Handbook of Indigenous education* (pp. 823–845). Springer.

Chalmers, D. (2003). Consciousness and its place in nature. In S. Stitch & T. Warfield (Eds.), *Blackwell guide to philosophy of mind* (Issue 2). Blackwell. http://www.consc.net/papers/nature.pdf

Christie, M. (2013). The box of vegies: Method and metaphysics in Yolŋu research, in M.Vicars, T. McKenna, & J. White (Eds.), *Discourse, power, resistance — Down under, 2*, (pp. 45–56). Sense Publishers.

Chomsky, N. (1979). *On language: Chomsky's classic works, language and responsibility and reflections on language*. The New Press.

Clendinnen, I. (2008, September 13–14). Inga Clendinnen on Black and White Australia. *The Weekend Australian Magazine*, p. 64.

D'Ambrosio, U. (1997). Ethnomathematics and its place in the history and pedagogy of mathematics. In A. B. Powell & M. Frankenstein (Eds.), *Ethnomathematics: Challenging Eurocentrism in mathematics education* (pp. 13–24). State University of New York.

Davis, B., & Sumara, D. (1997). Cognition, complexity and teacher education. *Harvard Educational Review, 67*(1), 105–125.

Davis, B., Sumara, D., & Luce-Kapler, R. (2000). *Engaging minds*. Lawrence Erlbaum Associates Inc.

Davis, B., Knight, S., White, V., Bell, R., Claridge, C., & Davis, S. (2001, March 4–7). *Use of arts in health promotion for Aboriginal women*. Paper presented at the 6th National Rural Health Conference, Canberra.

REFERENCES

Denzin, N. K., & Lincoln, Y. S. (2017). *The Sage handbook of qualitative research* (5th ed.). Sage Publications. (Original work published 2000)

Dewey, J. (1916). *Democracy and education: An introduction to the philosophy of education*. The Free Press, A Division of Macmillan Publishing Co. Inc.

Dewey, J. (2005). *Art as experience*. The Berkley Publishing Group. (Original work published 1934)

Dewey, J. (1963). *Experience and education*. Collier Books.

Dewey, J. (1989). *Freedom and culture*. Prometheus Books.

Eagleton, T. (2011). *Why Marx was right*. Yale University Press.

Earl, L. (2003). *Assessment as learning: Using classroom assessment to maximize learning*. Corwin Press.

Eliot, T. S. (1948). *Notes towards the definition of culture*. Faber and Faber.

Ernest, P. (1998). *Social constructivism as a philosophy of mathematics*. State University of New York Press.

Edmund, M. (2014). *Battarbee and Namatjira*. Giramondo Publishing Company.

Ellis, V. (2011). Recognising professional creativity from a CHAT perspective: Seeing knowledge and history in practice. *Mind, Culture and Activity, 18*, 181–193.

Engeström, Y. (1999). Activity theory and individual and social transformation. In Y. Engeström, R. Miettinen, & R.-L. Punamäki (Eds.), *Perspectives on activity theory* (pp. 19–38). Cambridge University Press.

Ernest, P. (1998). *Social constructivism as a philosophy of mathematics*. State University of New York Press.

Francois, K., & Stathopoulou, C. (2012). In-between critical mathematics education and ethnomathematics. A philosophical reflection and an empirical case of a Romany students' group mathematics education. *Journal of Critical Education Policy Studies, 10*(1), 234–247.

Freire, P. (1973). *Education for critical consciousness*. Seabury Press.

Freire, P. (2014). *Pedagogy of the oppressed: 30th anniversary edition*. Bloomsbury.

Friedman, M. (2002). *Capitalism and freedom: 40th anniversary edition*. Chicago University Press. (Original work published 1962)

Gillespie, A. (2005). G. H. Mead: Theorist of the social act. *Journal for the Theory of Social Behaviour, 35*(1), 19–39.

Gonzalez, N., Moll. L. C., & Amanti, K. (2005). *Funds of knowledge: Theorising practices in households, communities and classrooms* (1st ed.). Routledge.

Grant, S. (2016). *Talking to my country*. HarperCollins Publishers.

Grayling, A. C. (2021). *The frontiers of knowledge: What we now know about science, history and the mind*. Penguin Random House.

Groome, T. (1998). *Educating for life: A spiritual vision for every teacher and parent*. Thomas Moore RCL Company.

Hamilton, M. (2005). *We grow in the shade of each other: A study of connectedness, empowerment and learning in the middle years of schooling* [EdD thesis]. Australian Catholic University.

Hamilton, M. (2019). *Walking together to make a difference: A case study of Worawa Aboriginal College*. http://www.worawa.vic.edu.au/walking-together-to-make-a-difference/

Harvey, D. (2009). *Neoliberalism*. Oxford University Press.

Hooley, N. (2010). *Narrative life: Democratic curriculum and indigenous learning*. Springer.

Hooley, N. (2012). *Radical schooling for democracy: Engaging philosophy of education for the public good*. Routledge.

Hooley, N. (2015). *Learning at the practice interface: Reconstructing dialogue for progressive educational change*. Routledge. https://doi.org/10.4324/9781315724232

Hooley, N. (2018). *Dialectics of knowing in education: Transforming conventional practice into its opposite*. Routledge.

Hooley, N., & Levinson, M. (2014). Investigating networks of culture and knowledge: A critical discourse between UK Roma Gypsies, Indigenous Australians and education. *Australian Educational Researcher, 41*(2), 139–153.

Hughes, P., More, A. J., & Williams, M. (2004). *Aboriginal ways of knowing*. Paul Hughes Publication.

Indigenous Governance Toolkit. (n.d.). *Indigenous governance toolkit*. The Australian Indigenous Governance Institute. Retrieved November 25, 2020, from https://toolkit.aigi.com.au/

Isin, E. F. (2009). Citizenship in flux: The figure of the activist citizen. *Subjectivity, 29*, 367–388.

Jackson, P. (1998). *John Dewey and the lessons of art*. Yale University Press.

James, W. (1982). Introduction. In H. S. Thayer (Ed.), *Pragmatism: The classic writings*. Hackett Publishing Company.

Javier, R. A. (2010). *The bilingual mind: thinking, feeling and speaking in two languages*. Springer.

Jennings, P. (2020). *Untwisted: The story of my life*. Allen & Unwin.

Karmel, P. (1973). *Schools in Australia: Report of the interim committee of the Australian schools commission*. AGPS.

Kemmis, S., & Smith, T. (2008). Praxis and praxis development: About this book. In S. Kemmis & T. J. Smith (Eds.), *Enabling praxis: Challenges for education* (1st ed., Vol. 1, pp. 3–14). Sense Publishers.

Kimmerer, R. W. (2020). *Braiding sweetgrass: Indigenous wisdom, scientific knowledge and the teachings of plants*. Penguin Books Ltd.

Kincheloe, J. L. (2005). On to the next level: Continuing the conceptualisation of the bricolage. *Qualitative Inquiry, 11*(3), 323–350.

Langton, M. (2019). *Welcome to Country (youth edition): An introduction to our First Peoples for young Australians*. Hardie Grant Publishing.

Levi-Strauss, C. (1968). *The savage mind*. University of Chicago Press.

Lowe, K., Tennent, C., Guenther, J., Harrison, N., Burgess, C., Moodie, N., & Vass, G. (2019). 'Aboriginal Voices': An overview of the methodology applied in the systematic review of recent research across ten key areas of Australian Indigenous education. *The Australian Educational Researcher, 46*, 213–229.

Macy, J. R. (1983). *Despair and personal power in the nuclear age*. New Society.

Marti, E., & Rodreguez, C. (Eds.). (2015). *After Piaget*. Routledge.

Martineau, J., & Ritskes, E. (2014). Fugitive Indigeneity: Reclaiming the terrain of decolonial struggle through Indigenous art. *Decolonisation: Indigeneity, Education & Society, 3*(1), i–xii.

Matthews, C. (2019, December 5). *Indigenous perspectives in mathematics education*. Teacher: Evidence + Insight + Action. Australian Council for Educational Research. https://www.teachermagazine.com.au/articles/indigenous-perspectives-in-mathematics-education

Maturana, H., & Varela, R. (1980). Autopoiesis and cognition: The realization of the living. In R. S. Cohen, & W. W. Marx (Eds.), *Boston studies in the philosophy of science* (Vol. 42). D. Reidel Publishing Co.

Maturana, H., & Varela, F. (1992). *The tree of knowledge: The biological roots of human understanding*. Shambhala.

May, S., & Hill, R. (2018). Language revitalisation in Aotearoa/New Zealand. In L. Hinton, L. Huss, & G. Roche (Eds.), *The Routledge handbook of language revitalisation* (pp. 309–319). Routledge.

Merlan, F. (2009). Indigeneity: Global and local. *Current Anthropology, 50*(3), 303–333.

Milanovic, B. (2016). *Global inequality: A new approach for the age of globalisation*. The Belknap Press of Harvard University Press.

Mill, J. S. (1998). *On liberty*. Penguin Books Ltd. (Original work published 1839)

Morris, C. W. (1934). *Mind, self and society: From the standpoint of a social behaviourist. George Herbert Mead*. University of Chicago Press.

Murdoch, K., & Wilson, J. (2004). *Learning links: Strategic teaching for the learner centred classroom*. Curriculum Corporation.

Nakata, M. (2007). The cultural interface. *The Australian Journal of Indigenous Education, 36*(Suppl.), 7–14.

Nakata, M. (2018). Difficult dialogues in the South: Questions about practice, *Australian Journal of Indigenous Education, 47* (Special Issue 1), 1–7. doi:10.1017/jie.2017.22

New Zealand. (2006). *Bilingual education in Aotearoa | New Zealand*. Education Counts. Retrieved June 16, 2021, from https://www.educationcounts.govt.nz/publications/schooling2/school-networks/5075

Pascoe, B. (2014). *Dark Emu: Aboriginal Australia and the birth of agriculture*. Magabala Books.

Peeler, L. (2021). *Aboriginal change makers, Parliament of Victoria, Australia*. Parliament of Victoria – Education Zone.

Peirce, C. S. (2015a). How to make our ideas clear. In *Philosophical writings of Peirce* (Selected and edited with an introduction by Justus Buchler) (pp. 23–41). Dover Publications Inc. (Original work published 1955)

Peirce, C. S. (2015b). The essentials of pragmatism. In *Philosophical writings of Peirce* (selected and edited with an introduction by Justus Buchler) (pp. 251–268). Dover Publications Inc. (Original work published 1955)

Picasso, O. W. (2018). *Picasso: An intimate portrait*. Tate Publishing.

Piketty, T. (2013). *Capital in the twenty-first century*. The Belknap Press of Harvard University Press.

Pinker, S. (2018). *Enlightenment now: The case for reason, science, humanism and progress*. Penguin Random House.

Pring, R. (2013). *The life and death of secondary education for all*. Routledge.

Purdie, N., Frigo, T., Ozolins, C., Noblett, G., Thieberger, N., & Sharp, J. (2008). *Indigenous languages programmes in Australian schools: A way forward*. ACER.

Reay, D. (2017). *Miseducation: Inequality, education and the working classes*. University of Bristol/Polity Press.

Reyhner, J., & Eder, J. (2017). *American Indian education: A history* (2nd ed.). University of Oklahoma Press.

Reynolds, H. (2021). *Truth-telling: History, sovereignty and the Uluru Statement*. NewSouth Books (UNSW Press).

Sarra, C. (2011). *Strong and smart – Towards a pedagogy for emancipation*. Routledge.

Schleicher, A. (2018, November 12). *Educating students for their future, not our past*. Teacher: Evidence + Insight + Action. Australian Council for Educational Research. https://www.teachermagazine.com.au/columnists/andreas-schleicher/educating-students-for-their-future-not-our-past

Seigfried, C. H. (2002). *Jane Addams: Democracy and social ethics*. University of Illinois Press.

Settee, P. (2011). Indigenous knowledge: Multiple approaches. In G. J. S. Dei (Ed.), *Indigenous philosophies and critical education: A reader* (pp. 434–450). Peter Lang.

ShadowWalker, D. (2019). *Vygotsky and Indigenous cultures: Centuries of language centered learning*. http://www.u.arizona.edu/~deprees/finalpaper.pdf

Shay, M. (2020). *A flexible approach to learning: Can flexi schools close the gap for Indigenous learners*. https://stories.uq.edu.au/research/2020/a-flexible-approach-to-learning/index.html

Smith, L. T. (1999). *Decolonising methodologies: Research and Indigenous peoples*. Zed Books Ltd.

Spencer, W. B., & Gillin, F. J. (1899). *The native tribes of Central Australia*. Macmillan and Co.

Stanner, W. E. H. (1979). The dreaming (1953). In *White man got no dreaming: Essays 1938–1973*. Australian National University Press.

Taeao, S., & Averill, R. (2019). Tu'utu'u le upega i le loloto – Cast the net into deeper waters: Exploring dance as a culturally sustaining mathematics pedagogy. *Australian Journal of Indigenous Education*, 1–9. https://doi.org/10.1017/jie.2019.17

The Uluru Statement. (2017). Voice. Treaty. Truth. Uluru Statement from the Heart. https://ulurustatement.org/

Unaipon, D. (n.d.). *Coorong Country*. Retrieved June 16, 2021, from https://coorongcountry.com.au/david-unaipon/

UN. (2006). Report of the Special Rapporteur on the Situation of Human Rights and Fundamental Freedoms of Indigenous People: Mission to New Zealand, Economic and Social Council: New York. Retrieved June 16, 2021, from https://www.refworld.org/docid/45377b170.html

UN. (2008, March). *United Nations Declaration on the Rights of Indigenous peoples*. https://www.un.org/esa/socdev/unpfii/documents/DRIPS_en.pdf

UN. (2019, 22 April). *UN news. Human rights*. United Nations. https://news.un.org/en/story/2019/04/1037051?fbclid=IwAR14bvS-Twt2rYLYXzmz9bqTVTZ2XEdau7AoqBh6wF6ff_CuuAbO3W7WD64

van Gelderen, B., & Guthadjaka, K. (2019). Renewing the Yolŋu 'Bothways' philosophy: Warramiri transculturation education at Gäwa. *The Australian Journal of Indigenous Education*, 1–11. https://doi.org/10.1017/jie.2019.2

VCAA. (2021). *About VCAL*. Retrieved June 16, 2021, from https://www.vcaa.vic.edu.au/curriculum/vcal/Pages/index.aspx

Vygotsky, L. S. (1978). *Mind in society: The development of higher psychological processes*, (M. Cole, V. John-Steiner, S. Scribner, & E. Souberman, Eds.). Harvard University Press.

Wenger, E. (2004). *Communities of practice: Learning, meaning and identity*. Cambridge University Press. (Original work published 1998)

Williams, R. (1958). *Culture and society 1750–1950*. The Hogarth Press.

Williams, R. (1961). *The long revolution*. Penguin.

Willis, P. (1978). *Learning to labour: How working class kids get working class jobs*. Taylor and Francis Ltd.

Wittgenstein, L. (1921). *Tractatus: Logico-philosophicus*. Dover Publications Inc.

Wittgenstein, L. (1953). *Philosophical investigations*. Prentice Hall.

Wittgenstein, L. (1978). *Remarks on the foundations of mathematics*. MIT Press.

Yunupingu, M. (1999). Double power. In P. Wignell (Ed.), *Double power: English literacy and Indigenous education* (pp. 1–4). Language Australia.

Index

Aboriginal X, 7, 8, 12, 16, 17, 19–25, 27–36, 61, 62, 66–68, 71, 72, 85, 88, 89, 99, 105–111
Aboriginal and Torres Strait Islander 17, 23, 24, 88, 111
arts X, 16, 20, 23, 25–27, 32, 39–48, 60, 70, 71, 96, 111
assessment 4, 21, 23, 24, 26, 44, 76, 85, 86, 88, 94–96, 98
Australian Aboriginal culture 23

Battiste, M. 33, 66
bricoleur 102

Cadet Rangers 26
Canada XI, 62, 63, 66, 104
citizen education 91, 101–103
citizen knowledge 99
colonisation 4, 24
community/communities X–XII, 1–7, 9–13, 15, 16, 19–25, 27, 29–31, 33–40, 42, 44–47, 50, 52–56, 60, 61, 63, 65–71, 73, 76, 77, 79, 80, 84–89, 98–100, 102, 103, 108–111
consciousness 3, 4, 7, 12–15, 32, 33, 40, 48, 52, 64, 80, 92, 94, 95, 99, 100
culture IX, X, XII, 1–3, 8, 11, 12, 15–17, 19–21, 23–25, 27, 28, 31–37, 43–45, 50, 51, 55, 56, 62, 63, 67–69, 71–73, 76, 78, 84, 86, 88, 91, 93, 97, 100, 102–104, 107
curriculum X, XI, 1, 4, 5, 19, 20, 23, 24–28, 31–40, 43–46, 50–53, 56, 57, 62, 66, 69, 70, 73, 76–79, 85–89, 97, 99, 109

decolonisation 4, 5, 110
democracy IX, 10, 80, 85, 98
democratic classroom 85
Dewey, J. IX, X, 33–36, 45–47, 50, 82, 83, 85, 92, 98
dialogue 50, 72, 77–79
discursive curriculum 73, 86
dreaming 7, 22, 24, 27, 89, 106

education as philosophy of practice 72, 75, 91, 98
epistemology 29, 32, 36, 80
equality 6, 11, 14, 107, 110
ethnomathematics 50, 54–56

European Enlightenment 5, 12, 80

Freire, P. 50, 78, 79, 85
funds of knowledge 54, 68

Greek philosopher 5, 49
Greek philosophy 5, 15, 49, 72, 83

identity 1, 5–9, 21, 22, 25, 40, 54, 56, 71, 72, 86, 88, 107
Indigenous culture XII, 2, 3, 33, 34, 40, 91, 107
Indigenous education IX, XI, 16, 31, 37, 38, 75
Indigenous identity 1, 7, 8, 72, 86
Indigenous knowledge X, XI, 2–4, 24, 28, 32, 33, 57, 62, 105
Indigenous learning 75
indigeneity IX, 1, 3, 5, 7, 12, 15, 16, 19, 72, 94
Industrial Revolution 5, 12, 80
inequality XI, 6, 14, 15, 97
inquiry 2, 3, 33–36, 40, 49, 52–54, 60, 65, 73, 75, 76, 79, 83, 87, 89, 95, 96, 100, 102

knowledge IX, XI, 1–5, 7, 8, 10, 13, 14, 16, 18, 21, 23–38, 40, 43, 45, 49–58, 60, 62, 63, 65, 67–73, 75–89, 91–100, 102–107
knowledge exemplars 34, 36, 37, 75, 106

land 3, 4, 7, 9, 11–14, 16, 17, 24, 27, 31, 33–35, 37–39, 42, 46, 48, 52, 54, 56, 57, 62, 65, 71, 73, 91, 94, 103, 107, 108, 111, 112
language IX, X, 1–6, 8, 9, 11–13, 15, 16, 19–21, 24, 27, 29, 31–36, 39, 40, 43–45, 47, 50, 56–59, 62–72, 76, 78, 86–88, 91–93, 96, 99, 100, 102
language development 2, 27
law 11, 17, 19, 31, 101, 107
learning IX–XII, 2–4, 14, 16, 19–26, 28, 29, 31–36, 39, 40, 43, 46–54, 56, 60, 62, 66, 67–69, 73, 75–80, 83–89, 91–96, 98, 100, 101, 103, 106
learning from land 3, 33, 46, 54
liberalism 9, 10
lore 31

market 1, 6, 9, 14, 15, 79, 80, 94
market forces 80

INDEX

mathematics   X, 15, 16, 20, 26, 27, 33, 37, 40, 43, 49–60
Media Arts   25

Namatjira, A.   40, 42, 46, 71
Native Title Act   11
neoliberal   1, 5, 6, 10, 14, 19, 22, 33, 34, 46, 62, 72, 79, 80, 91, 94, 95, 101
neoliberal education   1, 34, 80, 95
New Zealand   XI, 53, 62, 68

Oral History Collection   109, 111

Pathways to Womanhood   22
Peeler, L.   X, 20, 21, 105
philosophy   IX, XI, 1, 2, 5–7, 12, 13, 15, 16, 28–30, 32, 40, 43, 46, 47, 49, 52, 56, 57–60, 62, 66, 67, 72, 73, 75, 77, 80, 81, 83, 91, 92, 94, 96, 98, 100, 102, 103, 109
philosophy of practice   40, 47, 49, 72, 75, 91, 98, 100, 103
Picasso, P.   40–42, 46, 71
polytechnic   25
practice-theorising   13, 79, 84
pragmatism   16, 29, 59, 67, 72, 75, 80–84, 100
pragmatist philosophy   X, 102
praxis   29, 36, 46, 47, 72, 75, 77, 83, 84

relationship to land   3, 7, 11, 12, 33, 38, 65
Renaissance   15

school community forums   21
school mathematics   33, 49, 50, 53, 54, 57, 60
secondary schooling   IX, 19, 20
self-determination   IX, 10, 11, 18, 91, 110
signature pedagogies   75–78, 83, 84
sovereignty   IX, 10, 11, 13, 17, 49, 93
Smith, L. T.   91
story telling   39, 44 45, 56
STEAM   26

theory and practice   63, 72, 75, 78–80, 83
Tractatus   58, 59
traditional knowledge   1, 2, 72, 98
two-way inquiry learning   34, 35

Uluru, Statement from the Heart   16, 17
United Nations   1, 10, 11, 31, 72

Vygotsky, L. S.   25, 63–65, 67, 69, 92, 99

Ways of Being   28, 29
Ways of Knowing   3, 15, 20, 28, 29, 33, 37, 38, 47, 87, 89
Ways of Doing   28, 30
Ways of Valuing   28, 30
Western scientific knowledge   2
Worawa Aboriginal College   X, 16, 19, 20, 22, 24, 25, 30, 35, 67, 72, 86, 99, 105, 110
Worawa Way   28, 29, 31, 35, 37, 75

Yorta Yorta   20, 68, 105 106, 109–111

Printed in the United States
by Baker & Taylor Publisher Services